The Music Makers

Let My Soul Surrender
Written by Rickie Byars Beckwith
Eternal Dance Music BMI © 2010
Rickie BB: Vocals/Electric Piano
Ricky Rouse: Guitar
John Barnes: Orchestration
(In Memory of Moonbeam)

One With the One
Written by Rickie Byars Beckwith
& Michael Bernard Beckwith
Eternal Dance Music BMI © 2009
Rickie BB: Lead Vocals/Electric Piano
Ricky Rouse: Lead/Rhythm Guitars
Georgia Anne Muldrow: Supporting Vocals
Sekou Bunch: Bass
Ndugu Chancler: Drums
Leon Mobley: Percussion

Main Line
Written by Rickie Byars Beckwith
& Michael Bernard Beckwith
Eternal Dance Music BMI © 2006
Rickie BB: Lead Vocals/Electric Piano
Ricky Rouse: Lead/Rhythm Guitars
John Barnes: Orchestration
Georgia Anne Muldrow: Supporting Vocals
Mortonette Stephens: Additional Vocals
Sekou Bunch: Bass
Ndugu Chancler: Drums
Leon Mobley: Percussion

Move Mood Interlude
Written by Rickie Byars Beckwith
Eternal Dance Music BMI © 2010
Rickie BB: Electric Piano
Chris Woods: Orchestral Arrangement,
Violin & Viola
Adrienne Woods: Cello
Sekou Bunch: Bass Solo

In God's Hands
Written by Rickie Byars Beckwith
Eternal Dance Music BMI © 2010
Rickie BB: Lead Vocals/Electric Piano
Miles Joseph: Lead Guitar
Ricky Rouse: Rhythm Guitar
Georgia Anne Muldrow: Supporting Vocals
Sekou Bunch: Bass
James Gadson: Drums
Ming Freeman: Orchestration

A Mighty Gift
Written by Rickie Byars Beckwith
& Michael Bernard Beckwith
Eternal Dance Music BMI © 2010
Rickie BB: Lead Vocals/Electric Piano

Heavenly Body
Written by Rickie Byars Beckwith
& Michael Bernard Beckwith
Eternal Dance Music BMI © 2003
Rickie BB: Lead Vocals/Electric Piano
Ricky Rouse: Lead/R̲
Georgia Anne
Vocals
Sekou Bunch:
James Gadson

About Robbi
Written by Rick
Eternal Dance M
Rickie BB: Lead Vocals/Electric Piano
Ricky Rouse: Lead/Rhythm Guitars
Georgia Anne Muldrow & Diva Gray:
Supporting Vocals
Sekou Bunch: Bass
James Gadson: Drums

Sanctified Mabel
Written by Rickie Byars Beckwith
& Michael Bernard Beckwith
Eternal Dance Music BMI © 2010
Rickie BB: Lead Vocals/Electric Piano
Ricky Rouse: Lead & Rhythm Guitars
John Barnes: Orchestration
Georgia Anne Muldrow: Supporting
Vocals
Sekou Bunch: Bass
James Gadson: Drums
Leon Mobley: Percussion

Discovery Interlude
Written by Ronald Stephan Muldrow
Courtesy of Sound Ground, BMI © 2011
Arranged and Produced by Ronald
Stephan Muldrow

Pure Agape Love
Written by Rickie Byars Beckwith
Eternal Dance Music BMI © 2009
Rickie BB: Lead & Supporting Vocals &
Electric Piano
Ricky Rouse: Lead/Rhythm Guitars
Sekou Bunch: Bass
James Gadson: Drums
Ming Freeman: Orchestration

Prelude In the Right Way
Written by Rickie Byars Beckwith
& Michael Bernard Beckwith
Eternal Dance Music BMI © 2010
Rickie BB: Electric Piano
Chris Woods: Orchestral Arrangement,
Violin & Viola
Adrienne Woods: Cello
Sekou Bunch: Bass Solo

Move In the Right Way
Written by Rickie Byars Beckwith, Michael
Bernard Beckwith, Georgia Anne Muldrow
Eternal Dance Music BMI,
Eristo̲   d, BMI © 2010
Rhythm Track
Vocals

Beckwith
Eternal Dance Music BMI © 2010
Georgia Anne Muldrow: All Vocals
Rickie BB: Electric Piano
Chris Woods: Orchestral Arrangement,
Violin & Viola
Adrienne Woods: Cello
Sekou Bunch: Bass Solo

Let My Soul Surrender
(Live Version 10.10.10)
Written by Rickie Byars Beckwith
Eternal Dance Music BMI © 2010
Courtesy of Agape International Spiritual
Center, Culver City, CA
Rickie Byars Beckwith: Intro. Piano,
Ricky Rouse: Guitar
Ming Freeman: Orchestration
Ben Dowling: Piano
Joy Julks: Bass
Rayford Griffin: Drums
Christian Klikovits: Keyboards
Idris Hester: Percussion

Project Advisor: John Barnes
Project Engineer: Larry Fergusson
Rhythm Arrangements: Ricky Rouse & Rickie
Byars Beckwith
Vocal Arrangements: Georgia Anne Muldrow
Recorded & Mastered at InnerSound Studios,
Los Angeles, CA

www.rickiebb.com
lovetrust@sbcglobal.net • 1.877.999.9802

A special note of gratitude is extended to John
Barnes and the staff and interns at InnerSound
Studios who make recording a delightful
experience; and to the Agape International
Spiritual Center, my spiritual home. The Agape
Community inspires me with the Real vibration
and that alone, has made all the difference in
my life. Thank you all so very much.

Published by

LoveTrust Media

P.O. Box 35779
Los Angeles, CA 90035-0779 USA
1-877-999-9002
Email: lovetrust@sbcglobal.net
www.RickieBB.com

ISBN 978-0-983404-20-0

Written, Recorded, Designed & Produced in Los Angeles, CA

Mixed Sources
Product group from well-managed
forests, and other controlled sources
www.fsc.org Cert no.
© 1996 Forest Stewardship Council

Edited by Kuwana Haulsey

Cover Painting & Inside Paintings ©2011.
Dudley Declaime Perkins • MySpace.com/dudleyperkins

Cover Design, Graphics & Book Design ©2011
Judi Paliungas, Susanne Abraham
PalimorStudiosDesign.com

Printed in China

A vibration
became a feeling,

A feeling evoked a thought.

A thought produced a mood.

A mood inspired the music

Music fashioned a verse.

A verse revealed what I or

somebody else needed to feel.

Rickie's music is vibrant
and organic, original rather than
prefabricated by the mind.
It is, in essence, a birth of
the eternal into time, evidenced by
how the hearts and lives of
her listeners respond.

Foreword

*I*t is my distinct honor to write this foreword to my beloved wife's latest expression of creativity – a new CD and accompanying book titled, *Let My Soul Surrender*, by Rickie Byars Beckwith.

Every now and then there is a soul who surrenders to the inner call of "go forth and multiply," or "create or perish" with such fierce resolve that their life is forever changed. Throughout all the years of her artistry, Rickie's passion to totally surrender to that creative urge has made her a finely tuned instrument for catching the sacred sounds and rhythms of the Eternal. I speak as one who has the joy of observing how Rickie lives her everyday life in attunement with her inner muse in such a way that brings forth songs of inspiration, gratitude, healing, transformation and celebration.

Rickie's music is vibrant and organic, original rather than prefabricated by the mind. It is, in essence, a birth of the eternal into time, evidenced by how the hearts and lives of her listeners respond. Individuals around the globe have shared how they have played her music during the delivery of a newborn, others how they got married to her celebratory songs, and entire spiritual communities use her inspired compositions as musical centerpieces during their services and special events. Simply put, people are healed and uplifted by what flows through Rickie BB, as she is affectionately called.

This new project is special. Of course this can be said about Rickie's entire body of creative works. But this one stands out as a statement about her inner evolutionary process: first as an individual dedicated to her growth and development, and secondly as an artist whose work is infused with her ever-deepening communion with the Source of her inspiration. The songs and the intimate background story that inspired each one speaks to the Magic that is everywhere present, constantly transmitting itself from every corner of creation if we pause long enough to humbly listen.

Rickie listens. She listens in dreams, during meditation retreats, in the mystical field of worship services at the Agape International Spiritual Center, in her seeming dark moments of angst and transformation and in moments of pure exuberance. With an artistic perceptivity she catches the "sound" heard by the inner ear and brings back to the village again and again a mighty gift of joy.

I'm compelled to say two more things: First, I suggested to Rickie that she write about the personal experiences which birthed each song, not only because I knew this would be inspiring to her many fans, but also because I am aware of her gift as a writer which also deserves to be shared. Secondly,

Rickie came into my orbit many years ago when a mutual friend gave a tape of her singing a piece they had co-written. While indicating that I thought the song was okay, I added that I wanted to meet the singer behind the song because I intuited something wonderful. It was a unique voice full of what I call "smoke" a soulful quality that transmits a healing frequency capable of touching people in a vulnerable, raw, profound way. The "smoke" still smolders in her voice, melting and healing the hearts of her listeners. Simply put, this woman can "sang."

It was the mystical Persian poet Hafiz who said, "Many say that life entered the human body with the help of music, but the truth is that life itself is music." From my professional and personal vantage point, it is easy to see that Rickie's life is a living testimony to his words. What a profound joy it has been for more than 22 years to walk the creative path with Rickie as a co-writer, a fan, a supporter, and a witness of her creative birthing process. I love this woman.

I now invite you to open your heart and Let Your Soul Surrender to real music as sung through Rickie Byars Beckwith. You just might be transformed in ways you cannot even imagine.

Peace & Richest Blessings,

Michael B. Beckwith

Michael Bernard Beckwith
Founder – Agape International
Author – *Spiritual Liberation*,
Fulfilling Your Soul's Potential
Husband of Rickie Byars Beckwith

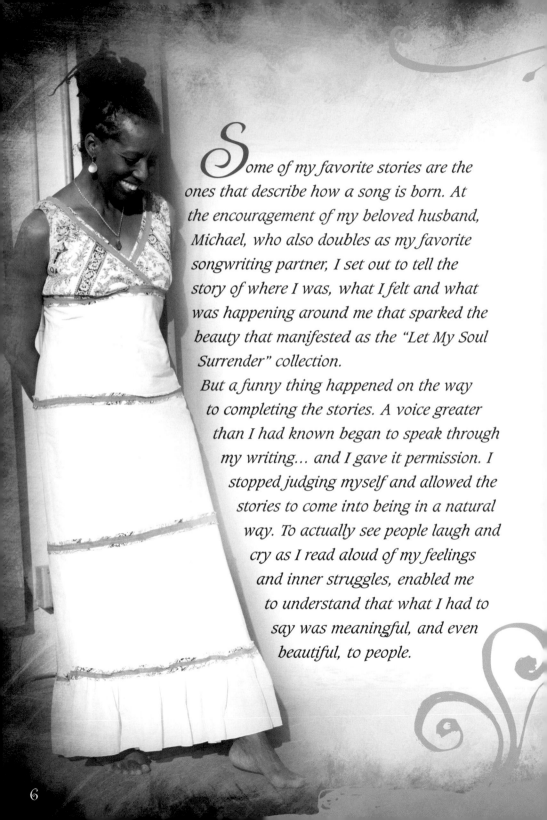

Some of my favorite stories are the ones that describe how a song is born. At the encouragement of my beloved husband, Michael, who also doubles as my favorite songwriting partner, I set out to tell the story of where I was, what I felt and what was happening around me that sparked the beauty that manifested as the "Let My Soul Surrender" collection.

But a funny thing happened on the way to completing the stories. A voice greater than I had known began to speak through my writing… and I gave it permission. I stopped judging myself and allowed the stories to come into being in a natural way. To actually see people laugh and cry as I read aloud of my feelings and inner struggles, enabled me to understand that what I had to say was meaningful, and even beautiful, to people.

Listeners were interested in the journey of each song and how it came to be. The stories made them feel better. But the real surprise was that the stories made my heart feel better. I had the best time, writing into the middle of the night, revisiting moments of inspiration that transformed my life.

And the lessons I gained from the completion of this music collection, with my first book of stories, are these:

1. Be yourself. Tell the story and let it go into the world to be what it shall be.
2. There will always be more to do and become, but there is nothing more glorious than to accept one's self, to trust the spirit inside and then – go for it!

With triumphant joy, I **Let My Soul Surrender**.

Rickie Byars Beckwith

Rickie Byars Beckwith

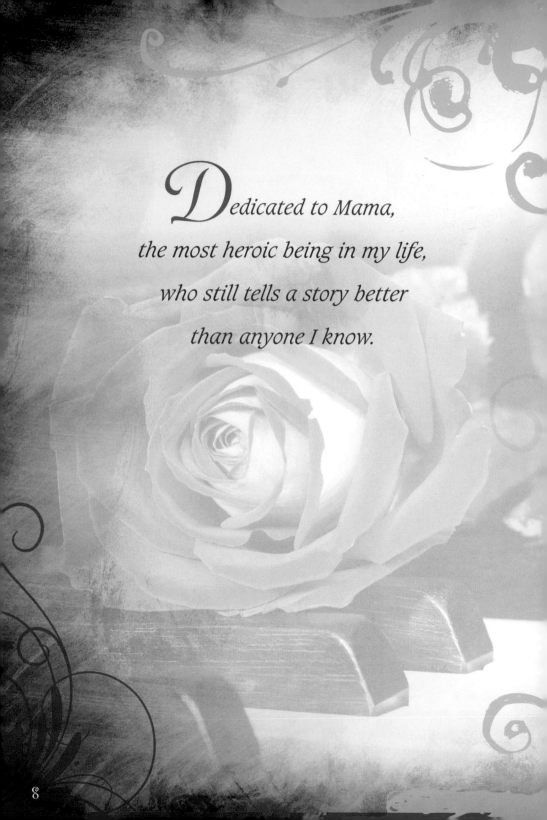

Dedicated to Mama,

the most heroic being in my life,

who still tells a story better

than anyone I know.

The Journey

Let My Soul Surrender

What am I to do, what am I to feel

I am like a child and you are with me still

What am I to do, what am I to feel

I am like a child and you are with me still

Listening in the silence, even in the sadness

Everywhere you are, oh everywhere you are

Let my soul surrender, greater I shall be

For what I came to do and what I came to see

Let my soul surrender, greater I shall be

For what I came to feel

Let my soul surrender to the heart of God

Let my soul, let my soul surrender

Greater I shall be for what I came to do

And what I came to feel

Let my soul surrender, let my soul surrender

Greater I shall be for what I came to do

And what I came to see

Let my soul surrender to the heart of God

Oh let my soul surrender to the heart of God

"Sometimes the worst day
for your ego is the best day
for your soul."

MICHAEL BERNARD BECKWITH

Let My Soul Surrender

A *song was sitting on my shoulder and I couldn't even see it...*

There's a sign for the Serra Retreat Center that you can see from Pacific Coast Highway as you ride up to Malibu, California. I'd passed the sign many times en route to a sweet little beach off the beaten path, just short of Zuma State Park. As Michael and I drove toward the sign and turned up the road that led to the center, I began to prepare inwardly for a mentally strenuous, yet fascinating, semi-annual ordeal.

Sitting in silent meditation for three days, observing my breath and thoughts, has never been my idea of a good time. But as Michael, my husband and Reverend, often says, "Sometimes the worst day for your ego is the best day for your soul." My resistance eased up a little when we pulled into the parking lot and entered the elegantly landscaped grounds, brimming with flowers and sunshine.

"The Catholics still know how to make stuff look good," I chuckled to myself.

IN ORDER TO MEET GOD

A stylish looking, elderly Monk in a brown robe walked ahead of us toward a meditation garden. My mind was momentarily flooded by memories of talent shows and youth activities that took place at the Catholic Church I attended growing up in Charlotte, North Carolina. But my resistance came thundering back at the thought that I might have to sit in a closed up room for three days in order to meet God, whom I could clearly see in the flowers and plants outside. Skeptical and petulant, these thoughts continued to grow in my mind as I walked into the dimly lit lobby with wooden paneled walls.

CHECK ONE, CHECK TWO...

"No sunshine in here," I mused cynically.

Imagine my surprise and gratitude upon entering the meditation chapel to find a circular, light blue room with floor-to-ceiling windows that allowed for a panoramic view of the ocean and mountains of Malibu. I decided that even if I continued to wrestle with my ego the whole time, the view before me was well worth the fight. Agape staff and volunteers prepared the chapel like busy bees on a mission to please a queen who obviously loved flowers, candles, Buddha statues and of course, incense. While Sese, the sound technician, searched her gear for her best wireless microphone, I watched how everyone worked together to decorate the room. Colorful fabric was draped around the windows. The piano and facilitator's chair brought flair and beauty to the space that felt sacred, even as I diminished the atmosphere with the usual microphone sound check, "Check One, Check Two..." Fortunately, Sese knew just how to work her equipment to make a voice sound warm and appealing.

The sweet little spinet piano, surprisingly nice and tuned, also felt good, as did the acoustics in the circular chapel. With my sound check complete, I was free for a moment to sit and be with my thoughts of what could happen in the next days of the retreat. *A new song might drop in... might not,* I pondered. But I quickly released myself from any pressure around delivering new compositions.

"I am here to lead chants," I reminded myself, "and to support the facilitator with musical accompaniment. Whatever happens after that will happen through the grace of God."

While the volunteers bustled in their beautification assignments, my ego bustled, not in preparation for something great to happen, but rather padding itself in the event that something great *didn't* happen. Somehow, this pre-meditation ego ritual succeeded in keeping my heart light and free of any obligation to create anything. When I felt all right inside myself, I left the meditation chapel to check out our living quarters, unpack my clothes and see what Michael was up to. About thirty minutes later, I returned to meet a room filled with attendees who shared their last conversations with each other before going into the silence.

WHY HAVE YOU COME?

Michael entered the room without ceremony, sat down in the draped chair and immediately began greeting everyone with questions. "How's everybody doing?" he asked. "Why have you come?" The second question received the liveliest answers. "We came to be better," some said. Others responded, "We came to shift our perception." Another favorite reply that I heard was, "We came to wake up!"

Some people were coming to the meditation retreat for the first time. Many had returned from years past for what had become a spring ritual. From far away continents like Europe, Australia and Africa, and various regions of the United States, folks had traveled to come and sit in meditation under the guidance of Michael Bernard Beckwith.

As my eyes scanned the room, it seemed that some folks were still dealing with question number one, "How's everybody doing?" And though the room was silent except for Michael's voice, the questions and messages written on the participants' faces came across as clearly as if they'd been spoken out loud. I noticed the strikingly sad eyes of an attendee who comes often to our meditation retreats and who seemed disappointed by something she couldn't seem to forget (or perhaps remember). Her eyes seemed to be asking, *"What am I to do... what am I to feel?"* Fortunately, a tablet was on hand so I scribbled down what I believed were her silent questions. Not too far from Sad Eyes, a young man sat with the hopeful eyes of a child who trusts that he will eventually find his way. He seemed to be adding, "I am like a child and you are with me still." I wrote down Hopeful Eyes' message as Michael continued to speak, setting the tone for all that was to come. Then I felt a group knowing, or perhaps my own, which echoed, *"Listening in the silence, even in the sadness, everywhere you are, everywhere you are."*

Michael's segue into prayer sent me on a scramble to finish writing my final thoughts. "Take a breath," he instructed. The attendees inhaled and converted the breath

into the sound of OM as they exhaled, becoming like a choir. It was soon time for me to offer a song or chant. As I rested the tablet on the piano, I gathered the courage to trust my hands to play chords that mirrored the feelings behind the words I'd scribbled down. The chords were slow to follow each other and had a haunting, yearning sound. I loved this song from the first chord and when I began to sing the lyrics, they did match the feeling in the room.

People had come, some from long distances, to sit and to find the answers to the questions that show up in their lives. *"What am I to do?" "What am I to feel?"* They wanted to find consolation in opening up, *"I am like a child and you are with me still."* They came with a song or dream or some great potential that I believe masquerades as resistance or restlessness when it's time to be still. But they, and I, were willing to try anyway.

And to think… a song was perched on my shoulder the whole time, waiting for me to get still enough to let it come through. Sitting with an intention to meditate allowed me to hear it. The whole dance of my seeming resistance culminated in what I consider to be the chorus for a lifetime:

Let my soul surrender and greater I shall be
For what I came to do and what I came to see
Let my soul surrender and greater I shall be
For what I came to feel…
Let my soul surrender to the heart of God.

*Let my
soul surrender
to the heart
of God.*

One With

Wanted to
feel something
moving in me

20

the One

(verse 1)

Wandering around, wondering why
I hit the glass with so much speed
What was I doing that I didn't see the glass
I was moving way too fast. I was moving way too fast
Felt like I was standing still, so I tried to gain some speed
With my mind and with my will
'Wanted to feel something moving in me
Moving like the fishes in the sea – rushing to get it done
Needing to be one with the One with the real vibration
Sweet liberation – rushing to get it done
Needing to be one with the One – with the One

(verse 2)

Working it out, she's wondering why
She married in such haste there was no way to know
That her dream of love was sweeter
Than the truth that came to pass
And a dream is still a dream
'Specially when you're moving fast
And she was moving way too fast

Felt like she was moving slow
So she tried to gain some speed
With her mind and off she goes
'Wanting to feel something deeper within
Deep like the power in the wind – rushing to get it done
Needing to be one with the One with the real vibration
Sweet liberation – rushing to get it done
Needing to be one with the One – with the One
One with the One – with the One

(bridge)

Fear is the villain planting lies of what we need
Real satisfaction comes in who we came to be
Like the air and sun and the earth we walk upon
Love is freely given and life becomes worth living
When we're one with the One – with the One
One with the One – with the One

(verse 3)

I'm watching the world and wondering why
We live our lives with so much speed
What are we doing – if we don't learn from the past
Are we moving way too fast
Are we moving way too fast, but really standing still
'Just trying to gain some speed
With our mind and with our will
'Wanting to feel something greater inside
Great like the river is wide – rushing to get it done.
Needing to be one with the One with the real vibration
Sweet liberation but we'll never ever get it done
'Til we become one with the One with One...

Needing to be
one with the One

One With the One

It was the twenty-fifth day of June, in the year 2009, four days after the summer solstice and the day that Michael Jackson died. What a very sad day it was for the world. A legend, a King, and a person I'd hoped to one day really get to know had slipped into Eternity. We never had the chance to meet in person but both times we'd spoken over the phone he had said to me that he looked forward to visiting our spiritual community, the Agape International Spiritual Center. And now, the youngest genius on the Detroit Motown label's roster of geniuses during my teenage years, who had brilliantly inspired the world, was gone.

Ironically, my husband and I were set to travel to Detroit that same evening. I'd never been to Detroit but, like a magnet, soulful musicians from the Detroit area seemed to find a way to me. It's no wonder that folks love the chants of Agape… they all have a great Motown beat, and are very often being played by musicians from Detroit! So I was already happy to be going to Detroit, and with the untimely passing of Michael Jackson, the trip had gained even more significance. Michael and I discussed the startling events of the day, while we packed our clothes, computers, vitamins and what seemed like a thousand additional things for a two-day trip.

Deeply engrossed in the conversation, we soon discovered that we'd lost track of time. The funniest show on earth takes place at our house just a few minutes before it's time to leave for the airport. Bedlam! Dashing out the door to the limousine (whose driver had been waiting patiently for us) we set out for the airport. We arrived at the airport 50 minutes before our scheduled departure, but by the time we got to the ticket counter the time had dwindled to 44 minutes. A very kind ticket agent delivered the disappointing news, "Sorry folks. Baggage must be checked 45 minutes before your scheduled departure." Michael and I looked at each other in disbelief. There was no way we could accept what she was saying to us. She continued, "Your reservations are gone. This flight is overbooked. I can place one of you in the number one position on the standby list for the next flight out at 12:30 am..."

ALL THINGS ARE WORKING TOGETHER FOR OUR GOOD

As the ticket agent tried to make sense out of the nonsensical way that airlines overbook flights, I found a little writing tablet in my purse and began to scribble, *"All things are working together for our good."* Our seats were gone and it didn't seem to matter that they were first class seats. Sure enough, Michael was able to get on the next flight, but it was clear, and only fair, that the fifteen names preceding mine on the standby list would take priority. I wouldn't be able to fly until morning but I was thankful that I could return home and not have to sleep in the airport.

Around 1:30 am, a car arrived to take me home. The

driver seemed to feel sorry for me and really made me feel better by listening to my story and adding his own two cents about how crazy it can get these days if you're late for a plane. I began to think of the benefits in having missed the plane as he drove through the quiet streets of Los Angeles. *"Well, I won't have to sleep through the night on a plane, I reasoned. I can sleep in my own bed."* I wasn't fond of red eye flights anyway and knowing that I would definitely make the 10:00 am flight, put my mind at ease. I said goodbye to the driver and entered my house alone.

As tired as I was, I never made it to bed because the sofa in the living room was so inviting. Without even undressing, I just stretched out on the sofa, which accepted me like an old friend. I covered myself with a near-by blanket and immediately drifted off to sleep. About five hours later, I opened my eyes to a quiet room, lit by the morning sun. After sitting in prayer for a while I went to my piano, across from the sofa. A succession of Motown-like chords played through my fingers while I remembered how Michael and I were rushing the night before to get to the airport.

WE GOTTA GO!

Those thoughts then brought to mind an incident that took place six years before, at a little boutique in Silver Lake, an artsy section of Los Angeles. It was my daughter's 21st birthday and I wanted to do something special for her but didn't quite know where to begin. Her 20th year had within it events that had been hard for us all. I just wanted her to feel my deep and abiding love but I felt awkward in knowing what to do. Parents of adult children know what I'm talking about. So there we were in the boutique when I realized that time had slipped away from us and it was so much later than I thought. I said to Georgia, *"We gotta go!"* and then attempted to charge out the door. But it wasn't a door. It was a glass window that fortunately did not break upon impact. However, my head felt broken as I dropped to the floor screaming from the pain.

Wandering Around

All these memories converged inside me as I played the first four chords. I began to sing in a tender Mary Wells kind of way, with the thought of Michael Jackson in my heart.

Wandering around, wondering why
I hit the glass with so much speed
What was I doing that I didn't see the glass?
I was moving way too fast. I was moving way too fast
Felt like I was standing still. So I tried to gain some speed
With my mind and with my will
Wanted to feel something moving in me
Moving like the fishes in the sea.

My heart felt light as I confessed my feelings. *"Rushing to get it done..."* But oddly, there were no tears or remorse for this was not a sad song. It was a triumphant flash back on a time when I was five years into marriage with a wonderful man, but still getting used to the changes and expansion that marriage can bring. My teenagers were growing into young

Real satisfaction comes in who we came to be.

adulthood while Agape also grew in leaps and bounds. In the middle of it all was a woman and artist, struggling to find a way to keep it real. The day I hit the glass, everything stopped and I began to slow down because I had to. In fact, for the next two years I couldn't handle any overload of any kind. I learned to take my time and to ask for help when I needed it and, of course, help was all around me. I just needed to slow down a little, take some time for myself and connect with the greatness in my soul.

RUSHING TO GET IT DONE

I actually finished the second verse before the chorus. The second verse speaks of a woman who married quickly but discovered, *"...her dream of love was sweeter than the truth that came to pass."* The final elements of the chorus and bridge came together later, with Michael by my side at the piano. As we sat together for, *"Rushing to get it done,"* Michael suggested, *"Needing to be one with the One."* The truth of those words hung in the air and we both felt the power like magic in the room.

I would hate to think that the Universe set me up to hit a

glass, witness the passing of a legend, or even miss a plane in order to write a song. I don't think it works that way. But an artist will take the elements of living, be they happy or sad elements, and allow meaning to emerge from them in the expressions of art. Michael and I were able to do just that with this song. Michael so beautifully delivered the words, *"Fear is the villain, planting lies of what we need. Real satisfaction comes in who we came to be."*

And together, we concluded this story with, *"Like the air and sun and the ground we walk upon, Love is freely given and life becomes worth living*

When we're one with the One..."

Main Line

(verse 1)

I need Spirit on the main line, pretty soon I'll be feeling fine
'Tighten up my connection, show me the way to go
I need a better understanding in a world that is so demanding
A world that is moving faster; feels like I'm moving slow
Give me Spirit on the main line, for a healing in my mind
I listen to the voice inside me, soon I'll be alright
Everybody say Holy (Holy) Spirit (Spirit) take me up to
(Take me up to) take me up to higher ground (higher ground)

(verse 2)

When Spirit's on the main line I am out of space and time
The love of God surrounds me, the answer is everywhere
Holy Elevation! I am one with all creation
The voice so sweetly speaking, the voice is always,
always there
Everybody say Holy (Holy) Spirit (Spirit) take me up to
(Take me up to) take me up to higher ground

(bridge)

Woooh I'm walking in pure intelligence, that is everywhere,
a realm of excellence
Praising the Spirit of the living God that is here and now,
wholly excellent
Woooh I'm walking in pure intelligence, that is everywhere,
a realm of excellence
Praising the Spirit of the living God that is here and now,
wholly excellent

All things are possible, in a pure intelligence that is everywhere,
closer than the air
All things are possible, in a pure Intelligence that is everywhere,
closer than the air
Hallelujah, Holy Spirit (Spirit), take me up to (take me up to)
Take me up to Higher Ground, Holy (Holy) Spirit (Spirit)
Take me higher (take me up to) take me up to higher ground
Holy (Holy) Spirit (Spirit) take me to (take me up to)
Take me up to higher ground

(verse 3)
I got Spirit on the main line, (yeah), and a healing in my mind
(Healing in my mind) Love of God surrounds me (well)
Now I feel alright (now I feel alright)
Hey y'all feel alright (yeah)
Tell me don't cha feel alright. (yeah) Hey when Spirit's on the
main line (yeah) We gonna feel alright (you gonna feel alright)
Hey! Do ya feel alright (yeah) Oh I feel alright (yeah)
Hey I feeeel (yeah) Yeah I feel alright (now I feel alright) OOOW
I feel alright (yeah) Hey! Do you feel alright, now (yeah)
Do you feel alright (yeah) Hey Hey
Now I feel all... I feel all right

M

ain Line was written eleven months before James Brown passed away. The Agape International Choir had been working on several solemn pieces with intricate harmonies that took a while to learn. As director and composer for the Choir, I decided to change up the energy and bring a soulful, more upbeat song to our repertoire. But I didn't want just any upbeat song. I wanted the song to be "funky."

When I awoke one morning with a desire to write a funky, upbeat piece, I had to go beyond my own natural writing style, which leans more towards ballads, popular music and chants. Funk, a complex system of rhythm and blues, demands a certain knowing in order to make it swing. And though I've been known to wail on top of some funk, I play my own Rickie style best and surround myself with talented band musicians who know how to make the music sound good. But now, the muse (or creative energy) seemed to be calling for something powerful, rooted in the funk. I needed some help!

THE GODFATHER OF SOUL

Faster than the thought of what I could not do or could not play, a vibratory alignment took place within me. My creative desire became harmonized with the energy of a funk master who knew how to get the whole world up on its feet. I'm talking about a brilliant man who earned his title as "The Godfather of Soul", Mr. James Brown.

In an instant, the living room became a stage and I was like James Brown, filling the air with a soulful verse, *"I need Spirit on the Main Line..."* But it could just as easily have been, "I need some funk on the Main Line." I started singing like James Brown, who danced like a god on fire and sang his messages with grunts in between the phrases. The first verse of "Main Line" ran alongside my memory of James Brown, who was full of confidence and not at all embarrassed to be himself. I made a demand:

I need Spirit on the Main line – pretty soon I'll be feeling fine
'Tighten up my connection – 'Show me the way to go
I need a better understanding – in a world that is so demanding
A world that is moving faster – 'feel like I'm movin slow.
Give me Spirit on the Main Line – for a healing in my mind
'Listen to the voice inside me – soon I'll be alright
Chorus:
Everybody say Holy (Holy) Spirit (Spirit)
Take me up to (take me up to)
Take me up to higher ground

The song had a force to it and when I sang the verse and chorus for my husband Michael, who was just returning from his gym workout, he could feel where I was going. As if he could hear the band playing every lick funkier than the last, he laughed, "Oh, yeah. That's it! That's It! This is a good one." He headed for the kitchen and I followed him, singing the verse again. While he prepared a green health shake for the family, cutting up fruits and soaking almonds, etc. I leaned on him to describe what happens when we are in sync with our Divinity. He measured green powder and Omega oils like the scientist he becomes every morning around the same time. Several moments later, Michael delivered a glass of delicious green shake and a pure account of what it means to be at one with God:

When Spirit's on the Main Line – I am out of space and time
The love of God surrounds me – the answer is everywhere
Holy elevation! – I am one with all Creation
The Voice so sweetly speaking is (the Voice that's) always there.

You just had to dance

When spoken, the words sounded more elegant than funky. But when I sang them they took on a different kind of power. I knew after a return to the chorus that the music arrangement for the band and the Choir would have to be tight on this song. Funk demands precision and I would continue to follow the lead of The Godfather of Soul, who didn't play around when it came to precision. James Brown created music and conducted the tightest bands in show business. You just had to dance when you heard his music.

His early songs, *Please, Please, Please*, and *I Feel Good*, were huge hits in our neighborhood. I was about ten years old when I first heard *Night Train*, a song that names the towns James Brown and his band, The Famous Flames, planned to visit on their tour of America. Leave it to J.B. to sing a traveling itinerary and make it sound good. I was excited that the Night Train was coming through Charlotte, North Carolina. It was the first time I'd ever heard our town

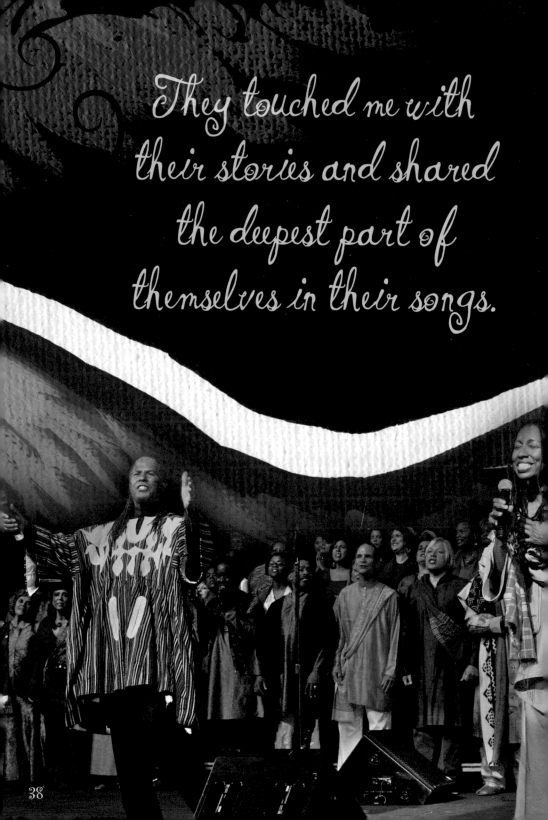

They touched me with their stories and shared the deepest part of themselves in their songs.

included on a song and it made me proud that James Brown remembered Charlotte. Actually, James said Raleigh, North Carolina, but it sounded close enough to Charlotte that I accepted it as so. In my little girl world, growing up in Charlotte, dancing on the front porch to the tunes that blared through our transistor radio, I'd imagine the singers of the songs to be my friends. They touched me with their stories and shared the deepest part of themselves in their songs. Nothing touched me more than to sing along with them.

LOVE SONGS

When it came to love songs, Curtis Mayfield of The Impressions was my favorite. In the song *Minstrel & Queen* he sang, *I'm not a king – I'm just a minstrel but could this really mean anything.* Truly, I could feel his pain over being a singer with no money, in love with a queen who apparently had lots of it. Poor Curtis made me cry for-real tears, cause I didn't have any money either. But who could cry for long in those days of eclectic radio programming? Something uplifting would usually follow a sad song. And when James Brown almost included my hometown on Night Train, we became fast buddies.

James continued to produce meaningful uplifting works well through my young adult years. If I was lagging, I could hear James screaming, "Get faster! People get faster," or "Make it Funky!" or "Get on the Good Foot!" And what a statement he made in the decade of the sixties when he cut his processed hair and went with his kinky natural, questioning the brothers with greasy do-rags, "How ya gonna get respect if you haven't cut your process yet?" And he did all this teaching on a foundation of funk music that I grew up listening to for most of my life. So it was incredible to discover that the funk was at my beck and call. I just needed some help – and James came from deep inside of me and "showed me the way to go." Michael and I finished the song quickly, with lyrics that rang true in every measure:

Wooh I'm walking in pure intelligence that is everywhere
A realm of excellence – praising the Spirit of the Living God
that is here and now, wholly excellent...
All things are possible in a pure intelligence
that is everywhere, closer than the air.

PLAY MY FUNK CHORDS

The writing of "Main Line" is a great example of what can happen when we call upon the Spirit with a receptive mind. In no time flat, funk was in my consciousness, or my inner house. I thought I didn't know what I was doing, but Spirit showed me how to feel it. Even in the studio when I laid down the rhythm tracks to "Main Line," Ricky Rouse – a great guitar player presently with George Clinton's premier funk band Parliament-Funkadelic, kindly showed me how to play my funk chords, "properly."

"It's not hard as you think," he coached me. "You wrote it! It's in you. You can do this!"

When I asked for help, help showed up everywhere. That's probably why James asked for help all the time... he needed it on and off the bandstand. As I listen to my studio rendition of "Main Line," it makes me think of great funk masters like Sly Stone, Stevie Wonder and even Parliament-Funkadelic. But it was James Brown who set the pace.

Four days past the winter solstice in 2006, The Hardest Working Man in Show Business was put to rest. Six days later, on the last day of the year and also "Choir Sunday," at Agape, I took the microphone and, with honor, made the following remarks, "This song is inspired by James Brown, The Godfather of Soul. James Brown, Thank you for everything you brought to us. This one's for you."

I NEED SPIRIT ON THE MAIN LINE!

The seven-piece Agape House Band began the intro and the Agape International Choir and I lit into *"I need Spirit on the Main Line!"* The

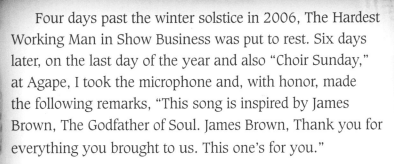

whole congregation was on up on its feet and funk was doing what it does. Maybe I'm sentimental, but it seemed that James could feel my heart full of appreciation for all that he brought to a little girl in the South who grew up to carry the funk in her own way. It seemed that he appreciated me just as much and joined me at the end of the song on the last words, *"Now, I feel alright!"*

Rest in peace, Godfather.

(verse 1)

Early morning invitation
Let a prayer rise with the Sun
Can my heart be free again
To live and love as best I can
And then place all things in God's Hands

(verse 2)

All too soon time advances,
All to soon I shall forget
Prayer at noon restores my heart
In the truth and strength a day demands
So I place all things in God's Hands

(bridge)

God is here and now
God will make a way somehow
Live to dream yourself awake
The path of Love will not forsake you

(verse 3)

Earth receives a kiss at sunset
Let my heart not miss the chance
To remember all is God
And live and love as best I can
And then place all things in God's Hands
Oh live and love as best you can
And then place all things in God's Hands

(vamp)

Creator of the Universe
How great you are
Oh guide me and inspire me to be
wonderful
Creator deep inside us all
You lift me up every time I fall
Oh guide me and inspire me to be
wonderful
Creator of the Universe
How great you are
Oh guide me and inspire me to be
wonderful…Amen

Oh guide me
and inspire
me to be
wonderful!

Ah...
thank you
God.
Hmm...
another
day...

46

In God's Hands

*J*awoke just as the first morning light began peeking through the space in the window curtains. Delighting in the beauty of a new dawn, I silently prayed, "Ah… thank you, God. Hmm… another day…"

My prayer of gratitude merged with a deep sense of wonder, which was all that remained of a dream I'd been having a few minutes before. The dream had been full of the sweetest, most heavenly music. It left me with a feeling of reverence for something I couldn't quite remember. In a desperate effort to connect the dots back to the dream and its music, my sleepy mind pleaded, "No… not yet, not yet… don't go yet!"

But of course, the dream faded. So I inhaled my reverent feeling, slipped out of bed and quietly left the bedroom. Like someone being called to fulfill an important assignment or destiny, I walked straight into the living room where my piano rests and sat down. My eyes closed as my fingers reached to play the first chords of the morning.

REMINDED ME OF COLTRANE

Immediately, I heard a celestial flourish of horns that sounded so pure, and yet so powerful. There was nothing I could do but surrender to those chords, which were clearly related to the feeling that had led me to the piano in the first place. I remember thinking, "John Coltrane would really understand what I'm doing." In fact, the reverential mood that the chords invoked reminded me of Coltrane, one of the greatest musicians in the history of Jazz.

So there I was in my familiar pose, in prayer at the piano just after sunrise, breathing in the fresh feeling that comes with a new day. The potential to love and the opportunity to see beyond my opinions of things inspired me to flow almost effortlessly with the first lines. Still basking in gratitude, I quickly saw that this song would be about the gift of prayer at sunrise, noon and sunset:

Verse one: *"Early morning invitation: Let a prayer rise with the Sun. Can my heart be free again…"*

Verse two: *"All too soon, time advances. All too soon I shall forget. Prayer at noon restores the heart…"*

Verse three: *"Earth receives a kiss at sunset, let my heart not miss the chance to remember all is God…"*

OKAY MOMMA…

I remember singing the first version for my young adult daughter. Georgia remarked with a sly grin (and what I considered to be borderline sarcasm), "Oh. It's about praying three times a day? Okay Momma…"

She probably liked it. But since she didn't kneel in reverence for the great piece I was uncovering, I took it a little personally, maybe.

Anyway, what's so wrong with a song about prayer three times a day? Or four or five? I wanted to ask her. But I didn't bother. Georgia knows how to stir the fire like an editor who won't quit. Undaunted, I set out to finish the song, which still sounded real good to me. However, I discovered that the completion of the verses wouldn't come as quickly as I assumed.

Altogether, it took three years for the entire song to be birthed.

BELIEFS

It took that long for me to finally understand that the song was not so much about praying three times a day as it was about my *beliefs* surrounding prayer. I'd always believed that one of the most sacred aspects of prayer was surrendering the individual will to Divine will, knowing that they are actually one in the same. To pray *God's will be done* is to surrender to that which is always seeking to express the best and the highest in any situation. However, my mind couldn't get past the fact that there were certain situations in my life where this didn't appear to be the case. It was like having puzzle pieces that didn't fit together no matter how you tried to arrange them. Eventually, I realized that the pieces would never fit unless I could come to terms with my disappointment at having been unable to shift some conditions, even with prayer.

During this time in my life, I'd had to stand by and watch as three very close friends of mine had passed away. Nothing I could say or pray made a difference in keeping them alive. Additionally, three young women from families I knew had been killed in three separate drive-by shootings. What good had my fervent prayers done to heal any of these situations? None, that I could see.

A Journey

"In God's Hands" became a catalyst that drove me to confront this impasse in my own thinking. It took me on a journey to release some of the confusion that I'd been harboring as a result of the experiences. After all, how could I sincerely write a song about the beauty and the power of prayer if, in my heart, I doubted the efficacy of my own prayers?

Piece by piece, I worked on the lyrics, checking with Michael periodically to see if what I was writing made any sense at all. Then one day while sitting at the piano, I remembered someone who modeled prayerful surrender so well, that the thought of him was enough to set the song on a course of completion. The being I speak of is Achok Rinpoche.

I first met Venerable Achok Rinpoche in the fall of 1999 in Dharamsala, India. Venerable Achok, Director of the Library of Tibetan Works and Archives in Dharamsala, is a personable monk, with a kind disposition and great sense of humor, in the order of His Holiness the Dalai Lama. I had the great fortune of sitting next to him during the sessions of the first Synthesis Dialogues convened by the Association of Global New Thought in 1999. The first experiment of the Synthesis Dialogues intended to gather great thinkers of our time with His Holiness to discuss solutions to the problems of the world.

Many times during the sessions, I simmered in frustration at the display of what I considered to be the narrow thinking and audacious egos of the presenters. Ven. Achok and about twenty-three others, including myself, were positioned to observe the whole process, but we were not to speak. When I would squirm in my seat or shake my head in disbelief at some of the questions that were being asked of His Holiness, Ven. Achok would smile and whisper to me, "Looks like we're losing. We have to pray."

PRAY HARDER

He was hilarious. After the first session, he returned with a gift of a beautiful Tibetan prayer bracelet for me.

"You need to pray harder," he said. He pointed at me and chuckled as he placed the prayer bracelet in my hands, "Here, these prayer beads will remind you."

At the time, I thought he meant I needed to pray for the others. As time passed, I began to see the deeper meaning behind his words. He was encouraging me to grow in my own compassion and patience. By "praying harder," by surrendering my idea of how the presenters should have been behaving, I could create a space of compassion that recognized the truth: that every person present was simply on their own path toward insight and discovery.

Seven years later, the congregants at the Agape International Spiritual Center had the privilege of meeting Ven. Achok Rinpoche at our Sunday morning service. They also had the opportunity to participate with him in an afternoon workshop. Dressed in his robe of crimson & gold, Ven. Achok presented his workshop to about four hundred people in our sanctuary. We all listened intently as he seemed to search at times for the right English words. This great Monk, who escaped from Tibet with His Holiness the Dalai Lama in 1959, spoke slowly and from the heart about the nature of compassion, consciousness and how he had spent his life on a journey of awakening. When Ven. Achok spoke of the Buddha, Jesus, the Christ and great teachers like his Holiness, the Dalai Lama, he raised his hands above his head, up into the air, and explained that these teachers were "waaay up there in consciousness." Referring to his own intelligence he said with tender reverence, "They are so much smarter than I am."

WAAAY UP THERE

He glowed with humility like I had never seen. While watching Venerable Achok, I could feel layers of judgment within myself begin to dissolve. Somewhere in my mind, I guess I'd believed that I was, "waaay up there," and that if I spoke my word with authority and believed deeply enough, I could receive the demonstration that I desired or manifest a healing.

However, years later, when faced with tragedy after tragedy, it began to feel as though my prayers were not having the effect that I believed they could or should have. All was not well in my mind. Questioning everything about my spiritual practice, the radiant faith that once inspired a song by the same title, had grown dim.

But just the thought of Venerable Achok brought a fresh gust of inspiration. His words, spoken very much in the way of his teacher and friend, His Holiness the Dalai Lama, echoed within me. They helped me to break through the impasse that had stopped me from completing my song. But more importantly, his words helped me have a breakthrough into a deeper understanding of the healing, mystical power of prayer.

In God's Hands

"Pray harder," Ven. Achok said. But not to change others. Pray for yourself to stay clear and to stay inspired to keep bringing your best to the day. *Early morning invitation: Let a prayer rise with the sun. Can my heart be free again to live and love as best I can and then place all things in God's Hands.*

"These prayer beads will remind you," he said. Take time to be with your thoughts and return to stillness. *All too soon time advances. All too soon I shall forget. Prayer at noon restores the heart in the truth and strength a day demands. So I place all things in God's Hands.*

"They are so much smarter than I am…they are waaay up there," he told us. I know that when I take this statement into my own heart, it does not diminish my intelligence. It enhances it. *Earth receives a kiss at sunset. Let my heart not miss the chance to remember all is God. And to live and love as best I can, and then place all things in God's Hands.*

For what its worth, I learned a lesson that I will probably learn over and over again. There will be things that won't go the way I want them to. I can't pray the world into being what I want it to be. But I can pray for myself and strengthen the muscles of compassion that will allow me to see the best of life. I can pray to stay inspired and joyously deliver the gifts I came to bring. I can pray for a lot of things, but the most effective prayer is the one of surrender, and not because I have been beaten down, but because I realize that there is an Intelligence that is, to quote a gentle monk, "waaay smarter than I am."

And I can trust in It.

GUIDANCE

The final chant at the song's end is almost childlike. I ask the Creator to guide and inspire me. Usually I would declare the truth and let it be, but this time, I allowed myself to ask for guidance, much like I used to do before I slipped into "knowing everything."

It felt so good to sing these words that were quickly written, as an afterthought while in the studio. When a chant as sweet as this fills my heart, I know something greater is at work, all the time. Let me always remember to trust in it.

"Creator of the Universe how great you are
Oh guide me and inspire me to be wonderful
Creator deep inside us all,
you lift me up every time I fall
Oh guide me and inspire me to be wonderful
Creator of the Universe how great you are
Oh Guide me and inspire me
to be wonderful... Amen"

*Oh guide me
and inspire
me to be
wonderful!*

A Mighty

Gift of Joy

(verse 1)

Trusting the gift within
Trusting in the love I know
I step with sweeter faith
Into the world I go
And in the day I have
Let there be time enough
Time enough
To bring a mighty, mighty gift of joy

(verse 2)

Move from the gift within
Move from the love you know
And step with greater faith
Into the world you'll flow
And in the time you have
You will be strong enough
Strong enough
To bring a mighty, mighty gift of joy

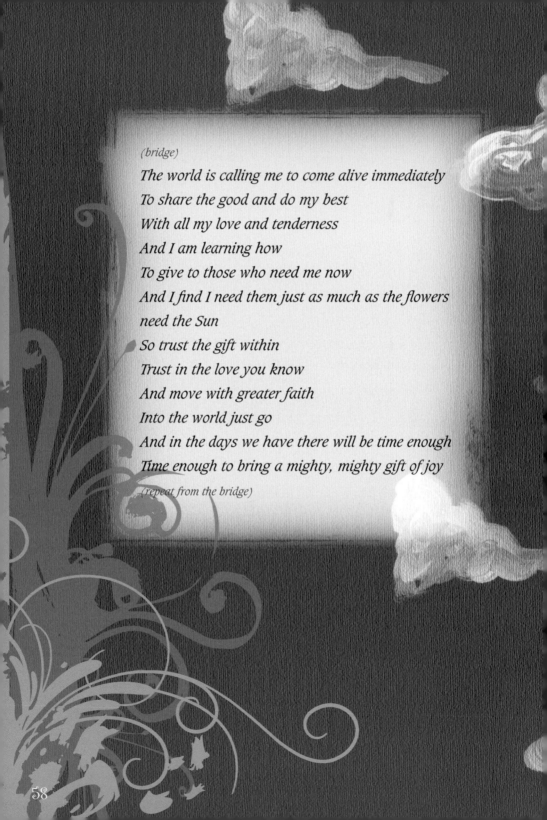

(bridge)

The world is calling me to come alive immediately

To share the good and do my best

With all my love and tenderness

And I am learning how

To give to those who need me now

And I find I need them just as much as the flowers

need the Sun

So trust the gift within

Trust in the love you know

And move with greater faith

Into the world just go

And in the days we have there will be time enough

Time enough to bring a mighty, mighty gift of joy

(repeat from the bridge)

59

*I*magine an invisible song spirit that can change into whatever sound or message needs to be heard in a given time. The song spirit needs a human voice in order to reach its full potential, and so perches on the shoulder of a child who will carry it, perhaps unaware, everywhere she goes. Imagine that the song spirit must wait for the one who carries it to find the space and wisdom to give it her devoted attention. It may take years, even lifetimes for the vessel to learn to listen to the message of the song spirit, but she eventually does. And the moment she listens, the Universe begins to dance. Then, like nature, the song spirit softly breathes into the heart, through the voice, and into the hands of its devoted vessel.

SONG SPIRIT

A new song creation begins to form as the vessel shapes it to be what it shall be. Pliable and willing, the song endures opinions and exhaustive rewriting until it is finally fully realized. It becomes a channel for the song spirit to speak to others of the beauty and excellence that lives within them. And what of the song spirit? Back it goes to its favorite resting place on the shoulder of its beloved.

Such is the message of "A Mighty Gift." This is a song that sings about its own destiny:

Trusting the gift within
Trusting the love I know
I step with sweeter faith
Into the world I go
And in the day I have
Let there be time enough
Time enough, to bring a mighty, mighty gift of joy

The song proved to be a mighty gift indeed, first to me and then to the more than 300 attendees who were present for its debut at the New Years Eve Meditation Retreat of 2009. The song carried a charge for me to be more accountable in all the ways that I could bring a mighty gift. I accepted the challenge.

GUIDANCE

Two weeks later, on January 13, 2010, the world began to see unbelievable images of devastation from an earthquake in Haiti that left the country in a state of emergency. The next day an international call for assistance to Haiti went out to the world and a local call came to me from a fellow congregant and dear sister friend, Catherine Scott, who is affectionately known as, "Scoti."

Scoti once lived in Haiti for several years while completing post-graduate work. Distraught at not being able to reach her friends in Haiti and wondering if they were okay, she said to me over the telephone, "What can we do? There must be something we can do... this is terrible. We have to do something!"

While listening attentively to Scoti, I continued to gather the final items I needed to take with me for an engagement in Denver. My flight would be leaving Los Angeles in two hours, and with a schedule already full to capacity, there was no room in my brain for clever creative measures. There was only one response I could think of: "I can sing. Maybe I could do a benefit concert."

RAISING AWARENESS

Scoti thought that was a great idea and suggested that I do a solo concert. But I thought the more folks we included, the better it would be. We would need to stick to a simple strategy with the intention of raising awareness and funds for our brothers and sisters of Haiti. Knowing how difficult it is to pull off a concert and how costly it would be to the church to pay the necessary personnel for their assistance, I did three important things. First, I got agreement from Michael, my husband and minister, that indeed a benefit concert could be done. Second, I called Rob, the facilities manager at Agape to see if he would be willing to help pull it off. He, in turn, got the whole media team involved and they all agreed to give of their services. Everyone replied a resounding, "YES!"

Next we called in Pat Finn, a television celebrity who also had friends who ran a children's hospital in Haiti. Pat signed on in a big way. Between Pat, Scoti, and a team of individuals who all wanted to bring a mighty gift to Haiti, we were able to collect, box and deliver tons and tons of medical equipment and hospital supplies. Finally, I called my assistant Tim to coordinate celebrity singers and musicians who came forth to participate in the benefit concert, which took place just four days after receiving Scoti's initial call for help. Celebrity like Chaka Khan, Howard Hewitt, Tina Marie, Brenda Russell and Niki Haris came to share in our humanitarian efforts. The Agape International Choir, the Agape House Band, and even my Mama Byars laid a musical foundation for greatness to happen. By the end of the benefit concert, which started at 3:00 in the afternoon and ended by 5:00 p.m., we had raised well over $40,000 in funds. After the concert concluded, a team outside continued to collect medical supplies that Haitian hands were happy to receive two days later.

Bring a Mightly Gift to Haiti

The theme we chose, "Bring a Mighty Gift to Haiti," was received with overwhelming enthusiasm. At the close of the concert, I sang A Mighty Gift and the words seemed to perfectly describe the collective feeling in the Sanctuary:

The world is calling me to come alive immediately
To share the good and do my best with all my love
and tenderness
And I am learning how to give to those who
need me now
And I find I need them just as much as the flowers
need the Sun.
So trust the gift within,
Trust in the love you know

Move with greater faith
Into the world just go
And in these days we have
There will be time enough
Time enough, to bring a mighty, mighty gift of joy

SONG SPIRIT

I don't know if you can imagine an invisible song spirit that can change into whatever sound or message needs to be heard in a given time. Somehow, I can imagine it. Maybe that's the reason it perches on my shoulder, and blesses my days on the Earth with songs of such amazing beauty. I sit in wonder about it all sometimes, and then I just go on about my business until the next time I am called to listen.

Time enough, to bring a mighty, mighty gift of joy

Heavenly Body

Heavenly body,
flesh this time

67

(verse 1)

Heaven body flesh this time
Born to love and born to shine
Heavenly Spirit flesh as me
Born to love, born to be free
Born to fly, born to feel
Born to cry and born to heal
Born to fly, born to feel
Born to cry and born to heal

(verse 2)

Heavenly body on the screen
What I desire in this scene is
To play the part I came to play
And spread some love along the way
Cause I'm born to fly, born share
Born to cry and born to care
Born to fly, born to care
Born to cry and born to share

(bridge)

Soul searching, soul searching
I know what made the stars and moon above me
Is deep within my soul and really loves me
Really loves you...

(verse 3)

Heavenly bodies, flesh this time
Born to love and born to shine
Heavenly Spirit, flesh as we

Born to love, born to be free
Born to love, born to be free
Born to love, born to be free, Amen, A-men
Soul Searching (searching in my soul)
Soul Searching (searching in my soul)
Born to fly...

Born to cry and born to share

My divine
assignment is to
anchor in the Truth
that I know,
which is far greater
than the facts
and/or fictions
that so often play
out in the news.

*M*ath is a description of how the Universe works. One of its most sacred uses is to reveal the truth of how things balance. Balance, especially for a double Libra like myself, is what life is about. Math is like Music. In fact, it is Music in the highest sense.

When I sit at the piano, I rarely think, *Hmm. This is a minor ninth chord with the ninth on top. This chord will be the vehicle that will allow my heart to open, because I've been so disappointed in my heart today. And the only way I am going to let go is to play this minor ninth chord with the ninth on top.* I don't think about it at all. Something in my imagination or thought is set into motion before I go to the piano. When I sit, my fingers begin to paint the way out of the lie I have accepted, or paint the way into the truth that needs to be known.

WAR ON IRAQ

"Heavenly Body" was written in the earlier part of 2003 when the United States government, under the command of George W. Bush, was about to declare war on Iraq amidst protests happening all over America and other parts of the world. Congress had decided that the only solution to disarm Iraq of weapons of mass destruction (which by now we know never existed) was to ship our sons and daughters off to a distant land with orders to kill other people's sons, daughters and families. We, the People, wrote letters, called our congressional representatives, took to the streets and even the beaches in protest.

Our outcry was dismissed as America invaded Iraq, not for the weapons of mass destruction, but for Oil. I remember weeping in Dallas-Fort Worth International Airport while watching the news reports of the invasion of Iraq. I just couldn't understand the inhumanity of it all and I couldn't understand why others weren't weeping too. Michael and I continued on our trip back to Los Angeles. I attempted to get myself together but I couldn't.

SUFFERINGS OF PEOPLE

I returned home distraught and overcome with remorse for the sufferings of African people, Croatian people, Tibetan people, Iraqi people, Native American people, enslaved and preyed upon people, and on and on. Everything seemed out of balance when I weighed the good I had tried to bring to the world, against the madness. All the music I had written, the choirs, the students, the tithes to charities, the vegetarian diets and hybrid car, none of it seemed to matter. So I did what I usually do in moments of great despair. I went to my piano and allowed the Spirit to speak to me.

Music provides the way for me to see through the appearance of things straight to the truth of what it is I bring to contribute to the good. My fingers went right to an A flat minor ninth chord with the ninth on top and continued through a maze of one major and then two minor chords. Clearly the tone of this song was introspective and filled with yearning. The questions "What can I do?" and "What is my true gift to the village first, and then to the world?" were answered as I began to sing:

Heavenly Body flesh this time, born to love and born to shine.

Heavenly Spirit flesh as me, born to dance, born to be free.

Born to fly, born to feel. Born to cry and born to heal.

SEARCH MY SOUL

The minor ninth, with the ninth on top provided an opened space for me to search my soul. The second verse formed with Michael, who always brings medicine or wisdom, by my side. *Heavenly Body on the screen, what I desire in this scene is – to play the part I came to play and spread some love along the way. Cause I'm born to fly, born to care. Born to cry and born to share.* And when the music opened to, *"soul searching, soul searching..."* I felt that I'd landed in the truth of who I am. I was able to proclaim, *I know what made the stars and moon above me is deep within my soul and really loves me, and really loves you.*

Regardless of what governments do, my divine assignment is to anchor in the truth that I know, which is far greater than the facts and/or fictions that so often play out in the news. I am here to love myself, to encourage my family, to nurture the Earth, and to joyously deliver the gifts that I get to bring to life this time. I usually discover the balance of life through the construction of a song and this song was no different. When the Math and Music of "Heavenly Body" balanced in the truth that what created us is deep within us and loves us, I could return to myself, stronger and better for the journey.

To Love and To Shine

Inspired again, I could urge others to love and to shine. I could remind them that we are *"born to love, born to be free... Amen."* "Amen," usually denotes the end of most songs or the conclusion of an "aha" moment, but this is not the case in "Heavenly Body." This song ends with, *"Soul searching... searching in my soul. Born to fly."* This means that we are born "to bring Eternity in to time" to quote my beloved Michael, and that is exactly what the writing of "Heavenly Body" allowed me to do.

I know what made
the stars and moon
above me is deep within
my soul and really
loves me...
really loves
you

About

Going home won't
be the same
cause Robbie's
not around

Robbie

(chorus)

What is it that you really miss about Robbie
What is it that you really miss about that girl
What is when you reminisce about Robbie
What is that you really miss about that girl

(verse 1)

Robbie was really cool, more like a friend than a sister
Yeah she was a real fool and maybe that's why I miss her
So much love and joy vanished from the town
And going home won't be the same cause Robbie's not
around

(chorus)

What is it that you really miss about Robbie...

(verse 2)

There ain't a person yet who could beat Robbie
dancing
Dragging on a cigarette, doing the James Brown
and jamming

Wooo, I tell you her joy could brighten up your day
And even now we wonder how could Robbie go away

(bridge)
And the hardest thing to do is letting go
When you love somebody, when you love somebody so...
And all around us there she shines
And all the time I'm thinking 'bout her...
Cause it feels real good just thinking 'bout Robbie
I'm just thinking 'bout her, Robbie
Just thinking 'bout her, just thinking 'bout Robbie...

(verse 3)
Robbie was really cool, more like a friend than a sister
Yeah, she was a real fool and maybe that's why I miss her
So much love and joy vanished from the town
And going home won't be the same cause Robbie's not around

(chorus)
What is it that you really miss about Robbie
What is it that you really miss about that girl
What is it when you reminisce about Robbie
What is that you really miss about that girl

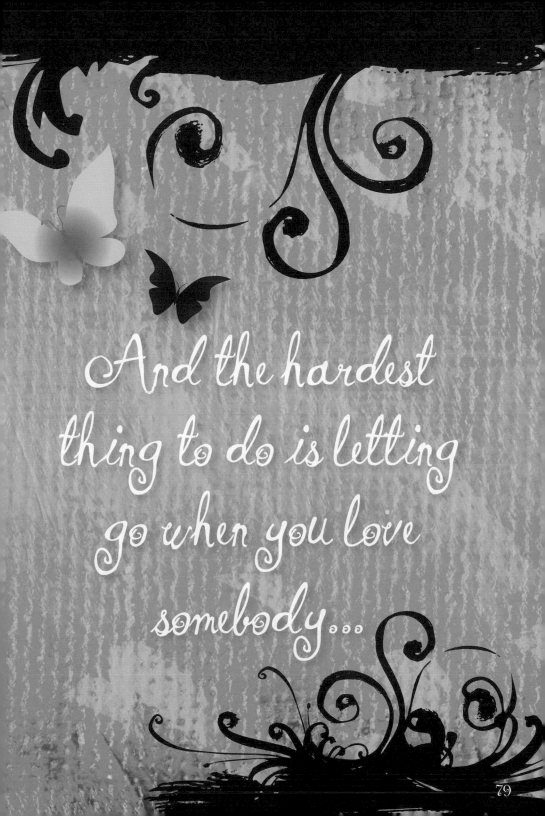

And the hardest
thing to do is letting
go when you love
somebody...

Robbie

The lyrics to "Robbie" were written in memory of Robbie Jones, the sister of a great singer and friend of mine, Tony Novell. I first met Tony in 1985 at a New Thought church where I played piano. He was about twenty-three at the time, a very good singer, and seemed to think that I would be the perfect person for a project he was working on. I welcomed the opportunity to make some money and quickly scheduled a time to meet with him at my home. A few days later, Tony came over to my house. But as he began to talk, I could tell that I wouldn't be making any money with this particular project. Tony had another agenda.

WHAT DO YOU MISS ABOUT ROBBIE?

His older sister, Robbie, a bright light in his family, had passed away and he wanted to honor her memory with a song. Not having the heart to say, *"Brother, I really need to be making some money right now!"* I listened to his plan. As Tony talked, his obvious love for his sister radiated through his words and touched me. When he said that I reminded him of Robbie a little bit, that did it. I got a pad and pencil and asked, *"What is it that you really miss about Robbie?"*

Tony answered that she was a lot of fun and kept folks laughing all the time. She smoked cigarettes and would have a cigarette hanging from her mouth as she danced like James Brown. He clearly missed his sister and for a moment I thought about what it would be like if I were to die at such a young age. Robbie had received a blood transfusion that infected her with the AIDS virus. Her death felt all the more tragic because it left her three young children, one of whom was only four months old at the time, without a mother. I had two small children myself. It moved me deeply to imagine what those little ones must have been through.

DANCER AND JOKESTER

So, after this very poignant and sweet conversation, I said goodbye to Tony and got to work. I finished the song quickly. It was easy to write and ever so delightful to sing. The notion of Robbie the dancer and jokester influenced the rhythmic pattern of the words. My favorite part was the bridge…

And the hardest thing to do is letting go, when you love somebody… when you love somebody so. And all around us there she shines… and all the time I'm thinking 'bout her, cause it feels real good just thinking 'bout Robbie.

When Tony finally heard the completed version of the song, he broke out into a radiant smile. And I knew why. The painting of Robbie, using music and poetry, preserved a precious memory of someone very special.

Robbie's song was a favorite request at "The Townhouse," my longest and last piano bar gig. Most weekends, the place would be packed with all kinds of people. Many were fans of mine who came to listen to my delivery of popular songs of the day, as well as songs that I'd written. Some folks just showed up to drink and socialize. There's no question that a singer has to be a good entertainer to keep a crowd's attention at a piano bar. Folks will talk back to you and let you know whether or not they like what you're singing. It's probably one of the most honest places in the world to get an opinion of a song. Anyway, when I'd sing "Robbie," folks would stop their conversations to listen to the lyrics and nod their heads in approval. Further evidence of the song's appeal would show up in the five, ten and sometimes twenty dollar tips they'd stuff in the big tip jar that sat on top of the piano. People cared for the story about somebody else's sister and listened like it was their own sister. For a few magical moments, the atmosphere changed to a living room and the audience felt like family.

LIKE A GREAT PHOTOGRAPH

One night, Tony Novell showed up at The Townhouse with two of his sisters who'd traveled from Chicago to visit Los Angeles and to hear me sing Robbie's tribute. At the first lines, *"Robbie was really cool... more like a friend than a sister..."* they closed their eyes and started smiling. And then their heads nodded to the beat with approval like the others at the piano bar frequently did. They cried a little and laughed at how accurately the song – like a great photograph – had depicted Robbie's essence. I loved every minute of being able to share in their memory of her. It was almost like I was an honorary member of the family and I was left that night with

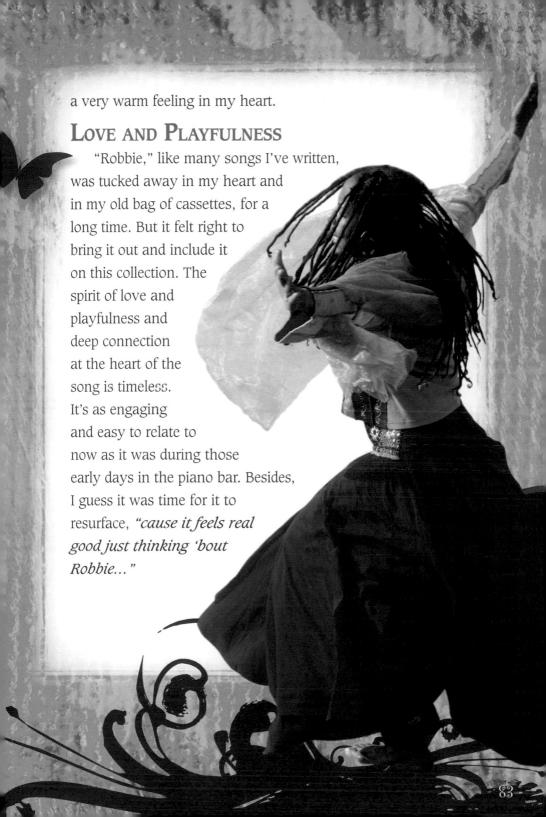

a very warm feeling in my heart.

LOVE AND PLAYFULNESS

"Robbie," like many songs I've written,
was tucked away in my heart and
in my old bag of cassettes, for a
long time. But it felt right to
bring it out and include it
on this collection. The
spirit of love and
playfulness and
deep connection
at the heart of the
song is timeless.
It's as engaging
and easy to relate to
now as it was during those
early days in the piano bar. Besides,
I guess it was time for it to
resurface, *"cause it feels real
good just thinking 'bout
Robbie…"*

Mabel

Sanctified Mabel

(verse 1)

This is a song about Mabel, sanctified was she
'Could bring a bad situation into a state of harmony
And when I'm feeling sad, when I feel I've been denied
I think about Sister Mabel
And try to see the world through Mabel's eyes
'Cause Mabel was sanctified

(chorus)

Mabel, say a prayer for me
Sanctified Mabel set my heart at ease
'Til I walk with a holy fire
'Til I draw the circle wider
There is so much more to realize
When I can see the world through Mabel's eyes
'Cause Mabel was sanctified

(verse 2)

She like a tall oak tree, she like willow that bends
And in a troubling time, she put a prayer in the wind
Mabel – a soldier for love, when I feel I wanna die
I think about Sister Mabel
And all the love that's streaming in her eyes
'Cause Mabel was sanctified

(chorus)

Mabel, say a prayer for me, Sanctified Mabel
Set the captive free 'til I walk with a holy fire

'Til I draw the circle wider
There is so much more to realize
When I can see the world through Mabel's eyes
'Cause Mabel was sanctified
(Ad libs)

(verse 3)
Troublin times, trouble in the land
Keep trouble on your mind
Gonna have trouble on your hands
And when I'm feeling sad, when I feel I been denied
I think about Sister Mabel
And try to see the world through Mabel's eyes
'Cause Mabel was sanctified

(repeat chorus)
Mabel say a prayer for me...

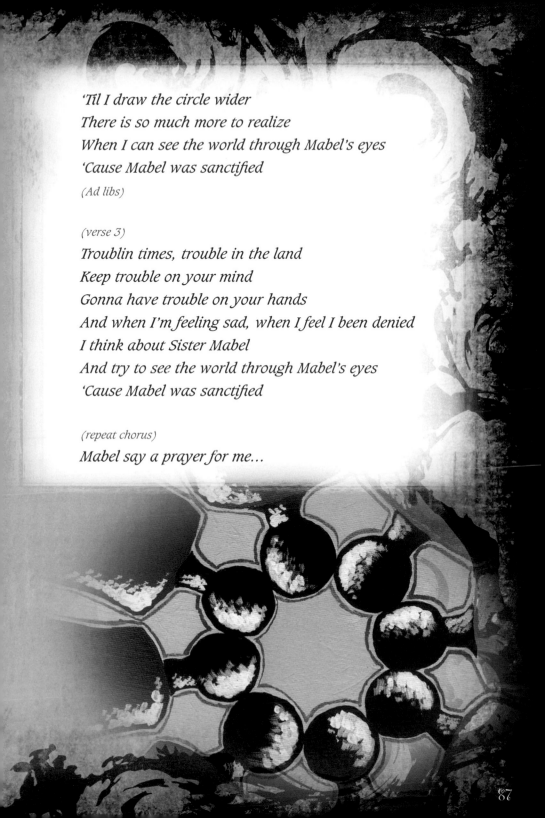

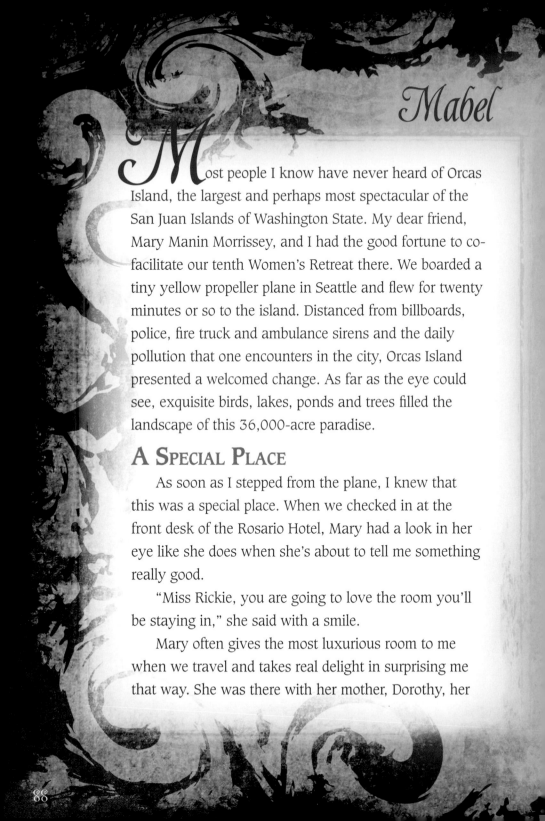

Most people I know have never heard of Orcas Island, the largest and perhaps most spectacular of the San Juan Islands of Washington State. My dear friend, Mary Manin Morrissey, and I had the good fortune to co-facilitate our tenth Women's Retreat there. We boarded a tiny yellow propeller plane in Seattle and flew for twenty minutes or so to the island. Distanced from billboards, police, fire truck and ambulance sirens and the daily pollution that one encounters in the city, Orcas Island presented a welcomed change. As far as the eye could see, exquisite birds, lakes, ponds and trees filled the landscape of this 36,000-acre paradise.

A SPECIAL PLACE

As soon as I stepped from the plane, I knew that this was a special place. When we checked in at the front desk of the Rosario Hotel, Mary had a look in her eye like she does when she's about to tell me something really good.

"Miss Rickie, you are going to love the room you'll be staying in," she said with a smile.

Mary often gives the most luxurious room to me when we travel and takes real delight in surprising me that way. She was there with her mother, Dorothy, her sister Jackie, her assistants (and good friends) Colleen and Karen, and they all got nice rooms. But I got the best room. I am always surprised and honored by Mary's generosity. As she opened the door and I stepped inside, I was taken aback by the stunning beauty before me. There was no back wall, only windows that revealed an elegant landscape of trees, mountainous terrain and a sparkling lake dotted with boats and birds. Mary smiled as I struggled for words to describe my feelings. The most I could say was, "WOW!" because the magnificent view had rendered me speechless.

"Writers frequently come to this island and this hotel in particular to finish their books," she explained. "Maybe you and Michael could come back here together, sometimes. It's a great place to rest and to write."

I FELT THIS ENERGY WELL UP IN ME

I did my best to take it all in. When she left the room, closing the door behind her I was wonderfully alone in a way I had never known. Mary wasn't gone two minutes when I felt this energy well up in me and I started to stomp my feet and clap my hands. Like thunder, the song erupted from me:

This is a song about Mabel, sanctified was she
Could bring a bad situation into a state of harmony
And when I'm feeling sad or when I feel I been denied

I think about Sister Mabel
And try to see the world through Mabel's eyes
'Cause Mabel was sanctified
Mabel! Say a prayer for me
Sanctified Mabel! Set the captive free
'Til I walk with a holy fire
'Til I draw the circle wider
There is so much more to realize
When I can see the world through Mabel's eyes
'Cause Mabel was sanctified

MABEL!

Just like that, alone in the suite for five minutes, I was lit from the inside out with a song about a powerful, praying woman. I went to the first session of the retreat and sang the first verse and chorus of the song before our intimate gathering of about eighty women. The women sang on the chorus, throwing up their hands and shouting, "Mabel!" This song, though unfinished, was already tremendously soulful.

Three years later, the song would complete itself in Los Angeles.

On the morning of the day I was to record the lead vocals for "Mabel," I asked Michael if he'd like to contribute some words. The song needed something else...

some more flavor. Though he was in the process of packing clothes for a trip, Michael stopped what he was doing and willingly offered the spice, *"She's like a tall oak tree. She's like a willow that bends."* I added, *"And in a troubling time she puts a prayer in the wind."* Wow! I love singing those words because that's what praying women like Mabel do.

Women like my mother, who many know as Mama Byars, and Mama Lissa Sprinkles, my spiritual mother, pray for me everyday. All the women on the Council of Wise Women at retreats I have been a part of through the years, wove the subtext for a song like Mabel. The Pulpit Women of Soweto, South Africa that I met in 1992 were like a council of "Mabels." Mostly consisting of mothers and grandmothers, The Pulpit Women held a mighty vision of freedom for all in their nation. In the days prior to the election of Nelson Mandela, The Pulpit Women would pray every week, for 72 hours straight for their families and children, some of whom had been killed for speaking out against the injustices of Apartheid.

Mabel, say a prayer for me

Mabel, say a prayer for me...
Mabel, set my heart at ease, till I walk with a
holy fire...
Pray for me until I can live in the truth.
'Til I can draw the circle wider.
Pray for me until I care for more than just myself
and until I can see beyond my narrow perspective.
There is so much more to realize
When I can see the world through Mabel's eyes
Cause Mabel was wise, and filled with compassion.
In other words... *Mabel was sanctified!*

This song happens to be my Mama's favorite and
I don't have to wonder why. It honors her and others
like her who have made prayer a way of life. Mabel,
"A Bad Old Girl," is the kind of friend everyone needs
to have – and the kind of woman I pray to one day
become.

She's like a tall oak tree.
She's like a willow that bends.
And in a troubling time she
puts a prayer in the wind.

Discovery Interlude

"Mom, I need to talk to you," said my 15-year-old son Stephan, while I was trying to take a little nap.

In those days, naps were a rarity for me. They still are. Musicians and composers, in particular, are known for pressing ahead until we fall out. I am slowly changing that pattern within me. But back then, a nap was a precious thing to take and I had no plans of letting mine go.

"Mom…" Stephan persisted.

He started shaking me. When that didn't work, he stretched out beside me. Stephan never did that. Obviously, this was a "momma help me" moment – and one that apparently deserved my full attention.

"Yes, son… whaaaat is it?"

As it turned out, Stephan wanted know what to do about the fact that his younger sister Georgia seemed to be better at doing "most things" than he was. When he took drum lessons, he had to study and practice the music, while Georgia didn't.

"Pops said she was a natural," he tenderly confessed. He went down a short list of things he loved to do and further lamented about how his sister out shone him at every point. Now the matter was filmmaking. He really loved it, but now she was trying to make films too.

"How do I handle that?" he asked. "She's so good at everything she decides to do."

I was surprised that he could express his feelings so well. My heart went out to him. I looked him in the eye and said, "I don't know what to do either."

He was right. His sister was a genius in her creative expression. Even at fourteen, Georgia had a whole lot of soul, on many different levels.

After thinking about it for another moment, I said to him, "Hey, you could be thankful that she's so wonderful and learn from her. Stop fighting her and learn to take care of her. Don't compare yourself to anyone but yourself and do your very best in all you seek to do."

It sounded like a lecture, but it was the most sincere and best counsel I could give at the time.

A TICKET TO LOVE

Over the course of three years, Georgia took a major leap in songwriting and music production. By the time she was nineteen, she had fully produced two albums of extraordinary music and soon found her work featured in magazines and music stores. While this was occurring, my husband, Michael, was also becoming more in demand for his wisdom and his voice in the world. To compare myself to them, or to expect my journey to mirror theirs would've been pointless.

We all have something to bring to the world. I believe that a gift or talent is given to us so that we may find a way to inspire others with that gift. A gift is not our ticket to ride – it is our ticket to love.

Eventually with the passing of years, Stephan's attention moved from video games into music and the expression of other aspects of himself. I recall that he was about twenty years old when I discovered he could play the piano. I'd thought Georgia had been playing, but the touch was different and the fingering was faster than I'd heard Georgia play. I walked down the stairs to investigate and there was Stephan, playing music that reflected my own types of harmony... but different. After that, I discovered that he'd also begun to try his hand at composing and producing electronic music. I listened to his music, encouraging him to continue, knowing that one day he would find his sweet spot.

Several years later, when he was about twenty-four years old, Stephan called me from his father's house.

Don't compare yours

"Mom, I got something I want you to hear," he said. "I think you're really going to like it."

DISCOVERY

Seven in the morning was pretty early in the day to be receiving a phone call from him. As I guessed, he'd worked through the night to complete the song that he wanted me to hear. When he came over, he handed me the CD with that big Stephan smile that uses all of his face. I put the music on and my eyes filled with tears. The sounds that had found expression through him were absolutely beautiful. To me, they reflected a certain understanding about what it meant to allow a gift to unfold. Creating the instrumental piece, entitled "Discovery," had been very good for his heart – and mine.

Since that time, Stephan has continued to expand his body of work and "Discovery" has been replaced with newer tunes in his repertoire. When I asked if I could use it as an interlude on my album, he said, "Of course. I would be honored."

But truly, the real honor has been to watch two teenagers grow into young adulthood while discovering the strength, integrity and focus it takes to express their talents. Indeed, they are well on their way.

Maybe now I can take a nap.

anyone but yourself...

Pure Agape

Llena me con tu poder cada hora
Llena mi corazon con Puro Agape
Eterno amor, para siempre
Llena mi corazon con Puro Agape

Love eternal,
Love forever,
Love unending

ove

(translation)

Fill me with your power each an every hour
Fill my heart with Pure Agape Love
Love eternal, Love forever, Love unending
Fill my heart with Pure Agape Love
Llena me con tu poder cada hora
Sana el mundo con Puro Agape
Eterno amor, para siempre
Sana el mundo con Puro Agape
Con Puro Agape, con Puro Agape
Fill me with your power each an every hour
Fill my heart with Pure Agape Love
Love eternal, Love forever, Love unending
Fill my heart with Pure Agape Love
Heal the world with Pure Agape Love
Free the children with Pure Agape Love
Fill my heart with Pure Agape
Llena me con tu poder cada hora
Sana el mundo con Puro Agape
LLena mi corazon con puro Agape
Fill my heart with pure Agape Love

La la la la
Sana el mundo
Llena mi corazon con Puro Agape

Pure Agape Love

Five agile fingers perfectly position themselves above the keys, as she plays the piano like someone who's studied for several years. Her dedication to producing the music she hears in her head reminds me of her father, who also discovered how to play the piano on his own.

These thoughts of Jada, my seven-year-old granddaughter, became vividly painted scenes that occupied my mind as I sat with an intention to meditate. Eventually, it dawned on me that my attention had been hijacked again, this time with proud thoughts of family. Inhaling deeply, I returned my awareness to my breath and to the place between thoughts.

Meditation often felt like a tedious practice for me, because the music and ideas flowing through my mind made me want to move and do something all the time. Imagine my relief when the meditation session ended and music could flow freely again. On this day, one of the last of 2008 at the New Years Eve Meditation retreat, I eagerly left the meeting room and crossed a grassy courtyard that led to a beautiful little chapel. I was no stranger to this particular chapel, that sat on the grounds of the Mary & Joseph Retreat Center in Palos Verdes, CA.

PEACE AND FAMILIARITY

It was still as quaint and lovely as the last time I'd been there. In fact, nothing ever seemed to change very much in this chapel. I suppose that in a world where things are changing all the time, this little chapel represented something very sacred, in that it had remained the same through all the years that I'd written chants there. Walking inside gave me a feeling of peace and familiarity that opened up a portal in my mind, which led me to a special place and time in my old hometown of Charlotte, North Carolina.

Unlike the chapel at Mary & Joseph, there aren't many physical locations that have remained the same in the town where I grew up. Most of my elementary schools and my senior high school have been demolished. Good Samaritan Hospital, that holy place where my mother delivered six of her seven children, gave up the ghost for redevelopment a long time ago.

The town square where the Second Ward High School Marching Band would show out at the Thanksgiving Day Parade is now a snazzy, chic place with restaurants and boutiques. The neighborhood drug stores and soda shops have all surrendered to the gentrification of yet another metropolitan city.

It dawned on me that my attention had been hijacked again

Since the early sixties, the population of Charlotte has more than doubled. This kind of expansion quite often brings with it, amongst other things, more stadiums for sports, more civic centers, merchandise marts, malls, the elimination of the old inner city and more traffic. The neighborhoods of Charlotte have changed so much that when I go home, I'm a stranger needing directions to find the streets I once walked with confidence.

Back in the day, the greatest teams in our communities were not the professional ones, because those didn't exist. There were no Panthers or Bobcats sports franchises. Instead, high school teams like the Second Ward Tigers, West Charlotte Lions, York Road Wapatis, and the Johnson C. Smith University Bulls were the teams that enlivened our community with their spirit and the African rhythms of their marching bands. We all reveled in the excitement of the homecoming games and their grand parades.

Untouched By Time

Unfortunately, much of this culture also shifted radically with integration and development. But there was something that remained somewhat the same through the years. For better or for worse, the church where I spent a good part of my adolescence has always appeared untouched by time, just like the chapel at the Mary & Joseph Retreat Center.

No matter how many years passed, entering Our Lady Of Consolation Catholic Church never failed to conjure up sweet memories from my childhood. Being there always brought flashbacks of my sisters and I singing under the encouragement of Mother Mary Dolorosa, with the assistance of a dedicated and musically talented couple, Mr. and Mrs. Davenport. The church kept us busy and inspired with talent shows, music for services and graduation programs, youth councils, girl scouts, and all the projects that brought so much joy and energy to our soulful church.

GREGORIAN CHANTS TO GOD

In a very real way these church-related activities shaped the person I am today. It's no wonder that my heart opens when I walk into any small Catholic chapel built in the 1940s or 50s. I remember with joy how I would stand outside the convent and listen to Mother Dolorosa lead the nuns, all African Americans (surprisingly similar to Whoopie Goldberg in the movie Sister Act), in their Gregorian chants to God. These women always dressed in traditional, floor-length habits of black and white, never showed their hair, and could show 'nuff sing. Dolorosa, the Mother Superior and lead singer, had the most exquisite voice of all. Her voice, in blended harmony with the other sisters, was more beautiful than any I'd ever heard. Throughout my adolescent years, the voices of those nuns inspired my soul in ways that would later be revealed in my own devotional chants to God.

For about seven years these Sisters of the Oblates (an order that originated in Baltimore, Maryland) exposed our community to another type of sound that totally differed from the Gospel, R&B and Pop tunes that flowed through the radio. The nuns left Our Lady of Consolation when I was about seventeen years old. About two years following their departure, I left Catholicism and Charlotte, altogether.

CHARLOTTE WAS CHANGING

The chapters of my life that included birth in a segregated hospital, growing up in the segregated south, worshipping in segregated churches and learning in segregated schools, were finally finished. Charlotte was changing and so was I. It was time to go and grow – to become the person I am still discovering inside, nearly forty years later.

My old neighborhood, my high school, and other buildings of Charlotte that mattered a whole lot to me may be gone. But the gifts planted by my schoolteachers, the community, the inner city where I grew up, and the nuns of my old church are vibrantly alive and continue to expand me in every measure.

These thoughts drifted through my mind as I looked around the chapel at the retreat center and then took my place at the piano. The melody and lyrics to "Pure Agape" appeared to me effortlessly. It was a beautiful chant that danced in the air. Written from devotion, and a yearning to be better in my heart, the music seemed to form from a place within me that was directly in touch with the innocence of my childhood.

Pure Agape Love

So, there in the chapel of the Mary and Joseph Retreat Center, I allowed my heart to open with adolescent devotion and I sang: *"Fill me with your power each and every hour. Fill my heart with pure Agape Love. Love eternal, Love forever, Love unending, Fill my heart with pure Agape Love."*

Overflowing with gratitude for the way the Spirit works, I sat in the chapel just a little longer, allowing the scenes from my childhood in Charlotte to fade into the sunlight that began to stream through the stained glass windows. The nine-year-old that stood outside the convent to listen to the nuns sing their prayers had become the woman who listened with the heart of a child for the harmony that is of God. It filled me with so much joy to listen in this way. It's the truest meditation for me and yields the highest gift… a song of devotion.

Rising from the piano and looking the room over one more time, I quietly left the chapel. The sun was high and shone brightly over the grassy courtyard and the heat felt real good to my body and soul. Everything feels real good when a song is born.

Later, I returned to the meeting room to sing "Pure Agape" to a crowd of people who were eager to listen. The retreat attendees loved "Pure Agape" right away and easily sang along. Several women, who were from Chile, Puerto Rico, and Costa Rica, helped to translate the words into Spanish and coached me in the proper way to enunciate the translated lyrics.

In a matter of hours, 2008 gave way to 2009. Through meditation and devotional singing, we anchored an intention to release the things that no longer served us and to celebrate the good of God.

Now, normally this would be the end of the story. But there's just one more thing to say. Rather mysteriously, I was recently led to open a binder at the bottom of a bookshelf in my office. Inside the binder rested a picture of myself at the age of seven, with a smile that spreads from ear to ear. The picture shows a remarkable resemblance between my granddaughter Jada and I. It's all that's left of any early childhood pictures of me. I don't lament this fact one bit because this one picture of myself is evidence enough to prove the kinds of things that grandparents just love to say. Things like, "She looks just like I did when I was a child!"

But Jada really is so much like me – so dedicated to producing the music she hears in her head. Maybe one day she will know the feeling of what it means to be devoted to the song of God. Maybe she already knows, and maybe that's why she recently insisted that I quit whatever activity it was that seemed more important than her, to sit down at the piano and listen as she played her latest discovery, "Pure Agape Love."

My goodness... what a wonderful world.

My goodness...
what a wonderful world!

Move
in the
Right Way

My eyes open, your eyes closed
You can't see the world that I behold
Let's move beyond what's right and what's wrong
Go to the center of where we belong
And move in the right way (in the right way)
Come on and move (let's move) in the right way
Hey move (move) in the right way (in the right way)
Oh let's move (let's move) in the right way

(verse 2)

If you're awake and I am sleeping
Meet me halfway cause I'm trying
And if the distance is a little too far
Move from the center of who you are
And we'll move in the right way (in the right way)
Hey move (let's move) in the right way
Come on and move (move) in the right way
(in the right way)
Oh let's move (let's move) in the right way

(bridge)

MOVE til our eyes open, DANCE 'til we come alive
MOVE 'til our hearts awake and DANCE out of time and
MOVE! We're a Mighty People! Move!
We are so much more

Let's move in the right way (in the right way)
Oh move (let's move) in the right way
Hm move (move) in the right way
Hey move (let's move) in the right way
Oh let's move in the right way

(verse 3)

My eyes open, your eyes close (closing)
You can't see the world that I know (I'm knowing)
If you're awake and I am sleeping
Meet me halfway cause I'm really trying (just to move)
Oh let's move in the right way
Hey let's move in the right way
Lets move beyond what's right and what's wrong
Go to the center – that's where we belong
From there we can move in the right way...

(ad libs...)

Move 'til our hearts awake and Dance out of time and Move!

Sad and stubborn, settled in my bones, ain't the way I'm growing old...

Move in the Right Way – Part 1

*S*ad and stubborn, settled in my bones, ain't the way I'm growing old...

It didn't take long after my mother moved in with us to see that she had a propensity toward neatness. Mama Byars holds a firm belief that there needs to be a certain order to things and she's passionate about things looking the way she wants them to look. For instance, after drying the dishes and cooking utensils, she will not be happy if you don't put the pots in the right place.

OH, LORD, HELP US

"Now, Rickie and Michael," she gently spoke in her first attempt to train us, "this pot goes here, and this pan goes down here... on this shelf... like this."

Oh, Lord, help us, I prayed.

For me, if the pots are in the cabinet, then the job is finished. I'd rather place my attention on other matters, and thus disregarded what she wanted me do.

I'm grown and this is my house, I thought, trying to justify myself. After all, she came to live with us!

But there was no getting around it. After a few years –
with lots of new pots and pans that she liked, glasses and
plates that she bought, swifter's and sifters that she just had
to have – the kitchen no longer belonged just to us. It had
become Mama's kitchen, too. And I had to admit that it was
so much nicer that way.

FLAVOR TO OUR LIVES

At first when she started making changes, it felt to me
like what we had wasn't good enough. But what she really
wanted was for us to live with a little more elegance and
efficiency in our home, which is now more beautiful for her
efforts. Mama brings flavor to our lives, and a usefulness
that allows me to focus on my duties at Agape and writing
projects. The turning point in my attitude came when I saw
how much joy it brought her to do these things for us. She
wasn't trying to run our lives. To the contrary, she'd become
an indispensible part of our lives.

And you'd better believe that Mama worked to become
more flexible and accepting of the way we do things, also.
When she first arrived to live with us, she was seventy
pounds heavier than she is now. She resisted giving up all
that meat she used to eat, but she did, finally. She chooses
a plant-based diet now, exercises, and engages in creative
endeavors that have produced a book and an amazing album
of her own.

In honoring the woman that my mother has become in

her eighth decade, these words, which I first wrote about myself, I now dedicate to her:

Sad and stubborn, settled in my bones, ain't the way I'm growing old.

Mama's response most definitely would be, "You got that right!"

Move in the Right Way – Part 11

Move! We're a mighty people. Move! We are so much more when we move in the right way...

"You can't hit me anymore," my eight-year-old son had solemnly said to me after receiving several pops on his behind for unkind and rude behavior.

"What did you say?" I screamed in disbelief at the audacity of him telling me, his mother, what to do.

This child has sho' nuff lost his mind, now! I thought.

SEEN AND NOT HEARD

I pictured my own mother and what she would do in this situation. If I, or any of my mother's children ever had the courage to say anything like that, we would have gotten twice the real whipping we were already getting. But that was in the era of children being seen and not heard; of children staying out of grown folks' business, back in the days when children got whipped with switches that they would personally have to pick from a bush or tree.

Where I grew up in the south, lynching, and hideous murders of Black people happened in for-real terms. A child saying the wrong thing at the wrong time could be dangerous for the whole neighborhood. So many of the old ways of discipline focused on keeping the child in his place. In the fifties, with the institution of slavery not even 100 years gone, a child learned his boundaries, usually through some form of corporal punishment, otherwise known as "a good whipping." Without a doubt my parents loved me and did their best to keep me safe. With honor, I wanted to do even better for my children.

I wanted to raise a liberated child, a child who could think for himself. I wanted my child to care for the rights of others, but to know how to defend himself when he needed to. Instead of whippings, I'd decided to dial down the violence to a mere spanking when necessary. Oh yeah, I had it all in place in my mind. But of course, children don't show up to fulfill our ideals. They show up as themselves. "They have their own thoughts," to quote Kahlil Gibran. Like an experiment in liberation gone bad, I now faced a child who felt free enough to request a change of protocol in my parenting.

YOU CAN'T HIT ME ANYMORE

It must have taken quite a bit of courage for him to muster the nerve to repeat, "You can't hit me anymore." He didn't raise his voice in the least. In fact, his tearful eyes seemed to show the frustration and emotional confusion that, perhaps, had led him to act out in the first place. It was as if Yoda, the wise old character from the Star Wars movies showed up all of sudden in this precocious son of mine who, two weeks later, would add yet another challenge to my diminishing

If the distance is too far, move from the center of who you are...

118

options of discipline: Stephan would invite me to "not scream at him, either."

"Huh?" I said.

Before I could say anything else, the words from a Sunday sermon popped into my mind: "You can't solve the problem at the level of the problem." Then my mind went blank, moving beyond the circumstance unfolding in front of me, into a much wider space of understanding and compassion.

WHAT HAD I BECOME?

What had I become? Suddenly, screaming at and hitting my children to get them to cooperate made no sense. The child raised the village that day, indeed, and set me on a path of loving that even today helps our family to heal the hurt from our past generations.

Many years have passed since then. Little Stephan has grown into a beautiful man and a wonderful, caring parent. He has long forgotten the day that I have always remembered, when he called me to rise higher, and to move in the right way.

If you're awake and I am sleeping, meet me halfway cause I'm trying. If the distance is too far, move from the center of who you are and we'll move in the right way.

Interlude for Nokware

The music in my dream rose up sweetly and serenely, as if a tone of Grace had floated through the ethers and found a resting place in my heart. I felt Nokware's presence beside me, breathing life into the melody that swirled all around us. And with acceptance that this beloved child would bring truth and joy to us all, I, the Grandmother, sang a song of him, as baby Nokware made his way into the world.

Illustrations by
Dudley Declaime Perkins

Dudley Declaime Perkins painted with acrylic on canvas. He holds associate degrees in Art History and Graphic Design. Dudley, a celebrated poet/MC, producer and recording artist, is the CEO of SomeothashipConnect recording label. Dudley is also the proud father of Nokware, Lil' Dudley and Ezra Perkins and is the loving husband to Georgia Anne Muldrow.

For more information visit:
myspace.com/dudleyperkins

Let My Soul Surrender

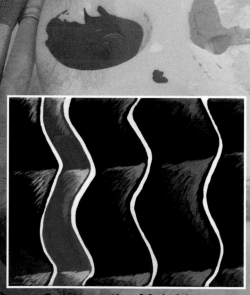

Spirit on the MainLine

A Mighty Gift

Heavenly Body

In God's Hands

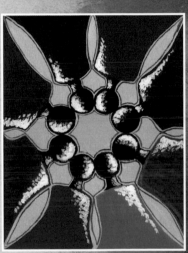

Sanctified Mabel

Move in the Right Way

Acknowledgements
The Book...

Many years ago, I found the courage to share an entry from my journal with a special being, whose presence, love and support had truly saved my life. I read the passage to my new friend Michael who proclaimed, "Ah! You are a writer... you have a real voice." I didn't quite know how to accept what he'd said, but somewhere, I believed him. **Michael Bernard Beckwith** is my beloved husband, my teacher, my favorite songwriting partner and greatest fan. He is the true love of my life... my person. Thank you, Baby. Your love is my shelter, now and always.

I thank my mother, **Mrs. Doris Houser Byars**, who first encouraged me to write my thoughts down in a journal. Her suggestion came shortly after I had eloped between classes, while attending Morris Brown College in Atlanta, Georgia. Mama, I think you knew I was in for a rocky ride and that my true voice would emerge through my journaling. As usual, you were, "waaay ahead of me." Thank you for my life.

I thank my editor for this project, **Kuwana Haulsey**, who allowed the best in me to shine and who truly inspired me with her notes of praise. Kuwana, I remain your most enthusiastic student. That one writing class I took with you is still well worth the investment. I'm ready for the next one!

I thank my daughter, **Georgia Anne Muldrow**, who invited me to consider **Dudley "Declaime" Perkins** to illustrate the songs and stories in this book. The way she said, "Dudley is the one!" let me know that she was not just being partial or sentimental toward her beloved. Indeed, Dudley Perkins was the perfect artist for this project. Thank you, Dudley, for trusting your enormous artistic talents again. Keep painting.

I thank my son, **Ronald Stephan Muldrow** who supported me every step of the way. Your tasteful eye in graphics, your willingness to show up in whatever capacity I needed and your overall respect for the whole project from the very start is appreciated beyond words. Thank you so much.

I thank **Shana**, **Rayshon**, **Estella**, and the team of **Kuumba** who listened, read, laughed and cried with me. Your thoughts were important and made all the difference in my heart. And thank you **Shana** in particular for your loving assistance on many levels.

Thank you **Crystal Roney** who showed up in the nick of time and **Rikk Galvan** who always answers my calls (oh yeah!). You are the one-two punch, elegant, efficient and so very necessary. Thank you for your guidance.

I thank **Mary Manin Morrissey,** my prayer partner, who kept me strong in my resolve to share my stories. Through the many years I've known Mary, she has seen what is true and real about me. Thank you Mary. You are a yummie good friend and I love you.

I thank **Judi Paliungas** for her taste in graphics and her masterful guidance for the book layout and completion. From the day of our first meeting, I knew we would make a good team and that we'd have fun together. The fact that she was already a fan of my music added even more spice. Judi, you really brought all the pieces together... thank you for setting me up to fly.

Thanks to the photographers and makeup artists (ooo **Arlene**... too much gloss!) who frame my face from their high thoughts of me. And thank you **SITA**, **Tina Preston**, **Jasmine Knauer**, **Carolyn Wilbourn**, **Angela Taylor**, **Dolores De Luce'** and all the fashion designers who dress me from head to ankle in the most exquisite clothes. Thank you all.

And finally, I thank those **friends and family members** of mine who encouraged me along the way, by listening to the stories and offering great feedback. The time we spent living and laughing through the stories was precious to me. Thank you so very much.

The Music...

At the invitation of John Barnes, a legendary producer and a great friend of mine, I began to assemble a collection of songs for this album project. I'd recently met **Ricky Rouse**, an extremely talented guitarist from Detroit, Michigan, who expressed that he loved the music I played. And so, with me on electric Wurlitzer and Ricky on the guitar, we marked the dynamic grooves for the songs that were so refreshing to my soul. When Ricky plays, you know something very special is taking place.

Under the careful gaze of **John Barnes** and **Larry Fergusson** (a great sound engineer and closet producer), we entered Inner Sound Recording Studios to record the album that was to become, "Let My Soul Surrender." The songs sounded so good, that my husband suggested I write the legend of how each song came to be, which I began to do almost immediately. But first came the sound.

I thank Ricky Rouse for working with me to anchor the feel of the music. **Chris Woods**, **Adrienne Woods**, **James Gadson**, **Sekou Bunche**, **Leon Mobley**, **Ndugu Chancler** and **Ming Freeman** contributed their instrumental musical talents. **Diva Gray**, a legendary voice in popular music (who sang on Robbie) and a vocal coach sent from God, helped to keep my voice strong and free. Thank you.

Then came **Georgia Anne Muldrow**, my precious daughter. Her unique sound and gift for vocals and vocal arrangements superbly supported my own lead vocals. She knew just what to do and how to do it. Thank you so much, Georgia.

After a few seasons passed, **John (Magic Juan) Barnes** prepared to wrap the rhythm tracks in an organic sound of funk and freedom. Like Georgia and Ricky, John brought joy to the music. And I just needed to say how much you make me stretch, John. I appreciate that about you… your honesty is a blessing.

From song to story, art and fashion, I thank these people in my life who honor what I do. I acknowledge you all for insisting that I be myself and for bearing with me as I continue in the discovery of just who that person truly is.

I acknowledge you all for insisting that I be myself….

Fashion & Photography

One with The One

"Paisley Bias dress," SITA Couture
Spring '11 Collection/www.SitaStyle.com
Photography: Shawn Keane/Photopoetry.Biz

Main Line

"Revelation," an Original Chartreuse Dupioni, Wilbourn Sisters
Design/WilbournExclusives.com
Photography: Barry Selby/BarrySelbyPhotography.com
Photograph of James Brown used courtesy of
Carl Studna/Carl Studna Photography

In God's Hands

"Rickie Inspired" **Photography:** Carl Studna
Carl Studna Photography
"White Winter Elegance," by Wilbourn Sisters Design
WilbournExclusives.com
Photography: Mikki Willis/MikkiWillis.com

Heavenly Body

"Boucle Audrey coat" over "Deep-V dress," SITA Couture
Spring '11 Collection/www.SitaStyle.com
Photography: Shawn Keane/Photopoetry.Biz
Photograph of Michael Beckwith
Mikki Willis/MikkiWillis.com

About Robbie

"Lavender Love," Original hand knitted sweater by
Dolores De Luce'/**Photography:** Michael Bernard Beckwith
"Twirling Nobantu," **Photography:** Courtesy of
Free the Slaves Foundation/freetheslaves.net

Discovery

Photography: Shana Jenson Muldrow

Pure Agape

Photography: Carl Studna
Carl Studna Photography
Photograph of Jada Selah Muldrow:
Ronald Stephan Muldrow

Move In the Right Way

"Rickie in Orange," **Photography:** Bonnie Schiffman/
Bonnie Schiffman Photography
Photograph of Mama Byars: Rickie Byars Beckwith
Photograph of a photo of young Stephan:
Ronald Stephan Muldrow

Interlude for Nokware

"Georgia & Baby Nokware,"
Photography: Rickie Byars Beckwith

Foreword Photography of Michael Beckwith:
Carl Studna/Carl Studna Photography
Closing Photography: Shawn Keane/Photopoetry.Biz
All other photos: Shutterstock.com

The Music of the Soul

My words cry out to give their hearts away:
Each has its story and comes from afar.
Willing carriers of private ends, they spend their
strength in missions not their own.

HOWARD THURMAN

The supreme life of Rickie Byars Beckwith serves as one of divine inspiration and upliftment. Often referred to as the First Lady of New Thought Music, Rickie serves as Music and Arts Director to the Agape International Spiritual Center and directs the Agape International Choir of 200 voices. Her profound mysticism demonstrates through her consciousness and commitment to service. This composer, songwriter, wife, and mother has made a tremendous impact throughout the world. The originality of her musical style emerged early in her life, as she learned from choir directors in the South and worked with leading singers and songwriters of the time. The foundation of her style ranges from gospel, rhythm, blues, and jazz. Yet, the true foundation and purpose for her work originates from the higher realm. She conveys the mystery of the Divine through the experience of her own divinity. Beyond mere skill or talent, this music demonstrates a life devoted to God, spiritual practice, and deep surrender. This salient nature arises because it is steeped in Consciousness. Unique in her capacity to express the symphony of the Divine, this prolific artist conveys eternal love and often compels one to inner contemplation, blissful reverie, and healing of the soul.

Through her music, we catch a glimpse of Rickie's sacred evolution and dual roles as planetary citizen and divine spirit. In the former, she echoes the voice of the Earth through songs such as "The Earth is Free Again" and "Child of the Sun". Here, she implants wisdom upon the fertile ground of one's being to a path of awakening. One notes her reverence for life, the appreciation for the planet, and the sacredness of our human existence. In the latter, we observe the Divine Spirit commanding our attention and uplifting the planetary vibration. In songs such as "Supreme Inspiration" and her rendition of "The Gayatri Mantra", Rickie calls upon souls to wake up. Such works are beyond mere "feel good" music, as they lift one into the higher realm. These vibrations course through the soul and allow healing, wholeness, and awakening to happen.

Alongside her husband, Dr. Michael Beckwith, Rickie has musically facilitated meditation retreats, workshops, concerts, and various events. The Beckwiths have traveled the world, inspiring souls and engaging hearts to a vibrant awakening. Her words are uplifting and her joy lights the room. Yet, the greatest gift that Rickie gives is that of humility and deep reverence for all of life. This radiates through her music, her service, and her countenance. Such commitment serves as a source of inspiration, as it imparts the gift of the Divine in the hearts of all who touch her sacred realm.

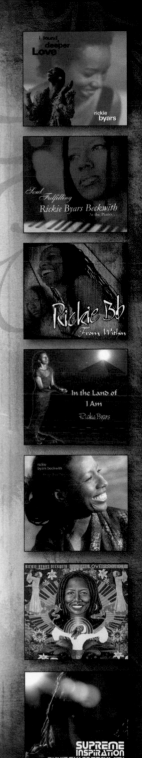

"There is nothing

more glorious

than to accept one's self,

to trust the Spirit inside

and then –

go for it!"

RICKIE BYARS BECKWITH

Let my soul surrender,

Greater I shall be

For what I came to do

And what I came to see...

Let my soul surrender

To the heart of God.